THE
INDWELLING
SPIRIT

ALBA HOUSE
a division of St. Paul Publications
Staten Island, N.Y.

THE
INDWELLING
SPIRIT

Robert W. Gleason, S.J.

Nihil Obstat: Gall Higgins, O.F.M. Cap., Censor Librorum

Imprimatur: ✠Terence J. Cooke, D.D., V.G.

New York, N.Y.—January 6, 1966

The Nihil Obstat and Imprimatur are official declarations that a book or pamphlet is free of doctrinal or moral error. No implication is contained therein that those who have granted the nihil obstat and imprimatur agree with the contents, opinions or statements expressed.

Library of Congress Catalog Card Number: 66-19719

Designed, printed and bound in the U.S.A. by the Pauline Fathers and Brothers of the Society of St. Paul as a part of their Communications Apostolate.

CONTENTS

Chapter

Page

1. Revelation and the Divine Indwelling   1

2. Revelation and the Divine Indwelling   12

3. Formal Causality and the Greek Fathers   21

4. The Union of Friendship   38

5. Objective Union   45

6. The Production of Grace   59

7. The Theory of Scheeben   72

8. De la Taille's Theory   79

9. Objections and Replies   94

10. The Value of de la Taille's Theory   107

Chapter 1.   Revelation and the
Divine Indwelling

WHAT does revelation tell us about the indwelling of the Holy Trinity in the soul of the just man? Reviewing the proofs for the fact of the indwelling, we shall attempt to disengage the information that the sources of revelation provide concerning the nature of the indwelling, its mode, and the kind of causality which is at work to create such an indwelling.

Any explanation of the mode of the indwelling must fit the facts of revelation. In order to evaluate the various theories which attempt an explanation of the theological problem of the mode of the divine indwelling, it is first necessary to isolate and organize the truths of revelation intimately connected with the problem. Revelation does not contain the solution of the problem, but it provides us with the elements of the problem. Before we can undertake to clarify and organize, in philosophical terms, what our faith teaches us concerning the mode of the divine indwelling we must have on hand the data of faith and of theology concerning the indwelling.

To imagine that revelation teaches nothing more than the bare fact of the indwelling would be to err. Revelation also sets certain limits to our speculation about the nature of the indwelling. It tells us clearly under what conditions the indwelling takes place. It gives us certain indications which will serve as at least negative norms. Any attempt systematically to explain the nature of the divine indwelling which contradicts the clear indications of revelation would have to be rejected as false.

Revelation makes it clear that the divine indwelling can be spoken of only with regard to souls in the state of sanctifying grace. This can be discerned clearly in the fourteenth chapter of St. John: "Jesus answered him, 'If a man loves me, he will keep my word, and my Father will love him, and we will come to him and make our home with him.'" To those who love will be given a new presence of the beloved.

Just before this, in verse sixteen, Christ had promised to his Apostles that he would ask the Father and the Father would give them another Counselor (Advocate or Paraclete) who would remain with them "forever." Again a new presence is spoken of and again the connection with charity is clear from the seventeenth verse. The Apostles love Christ and to those who love will be sent the Holy Spirit, who will remain with them permanently: "Even the Spirit of truth, whom the world cannot receive, because it neither sees him nor knows him; you know him, for he dwells with you, and will be in you." In the context there is no question of first justification, but this is presupposed, since Christ is speaking to the Apostles who are already justified. In the twenty-third verse, the inhabitation is promised to all who love Christ and keep his commandments. To these just the Holy Spirit will be given; to these will come the Father and Son in a new way, for if they come to those who love they may be said to have been in some way previously absent to them.

This emphasis on the fact that it is to the just that the Holy Trinity come in this new way is continued in St. Paul. In the first Epistle to the Corinthians, Chapter the sixth, verse nineteen, he says, "Do you not know that your body is a temple of the Holy Spirit within you, which you have from God? You are not your own; you were bought with a price." It seems to be clear from the exhortation of St. Paul that he is addressing those who may be supposed to have been justified, to be in Christ; for this reason he urges them to live in accordance with their Christian liberty and to remember that and avoid those sins which drive out the indwelling Spirit. In verse eleven he exhorts them to remember that they have passed out of the state of servitude to sin: "And such were some of you. But you were washed, you were sanctified, you were justified in the name of the Lord Jesus Christ and in the Spirit of our God." It is to these justified souls that St. Paul addresses the message of the inhabiting Spirit of verse seventeen.

Again in Romans, verse five of chapter five, Paul tells the Christians: "And hope does not disappoint us, because God's love has been poured into our hearts through the Holy Spirit who has been given to us." The point stands: the Holy Spirit is given to the just intrinsically, as a gratuitous effect of the redemptive sacrifice of Christ.

Again in Romans, verses nine and ten of chapter eight, the Romans are said to be "in the Spirit", that is, to be under the influence of the Holy Spirit in the nobler part of their soul, providing they possess the Holy Spirit. The connection between grace and the divine in-habitation is very close in this passage; one has the Holy Spirit and lives under the influence of grace, or else one is simply unregenerate, "in the flesh." The just man is just insofar as he possesses the Holy Spirit.

This connection between justification and the sending of the Holy Spirit could hardly be closer than in Galatians, chapter four, verse six: "And because you are sons, God has sent the Spirit of his Son into our hearts, crying, 'Abba! Father!' ". Another brief expression of the in-timate relation between charity and the Gift of the Holy Spirit is found in the First Letter of John, chapter four, verse sixteen: "God is love, and he who abides in love abides in God, and God abides in him."

This is also the doctrine of the Church Fathers who teach that at Baptism the soul receives the Holy Spirit,[1] and that they alone are just who maintain unity with the Holy Spirit given in Baptism. Ignatius of Antioch calls the faithful "God-bearers" and "Christ-bearers."[2] We who have received the remission of sins and are renewed in the hope of the Lord are entirely recreated; therefore God truly dwells within us.[3] In his own way, Tatian affirms the same thing.[4]

St. Augustine says peremptorily: "We must confess that if God be everywhere by His Divinity, he is not everywhere by the grace of the Inhabitation . . . One cannot apply to all the words of the Apostle: Know you not that you are the temples of the Holy Spirit, that the Spirit of God dwells in you. On the contrary it must be said of some: He who has not the Spirit of Jesus Christ, he does not belong to Jesus Christ."[5]

St. Cyril of Alexandria states: "If we have not the Spirit within us we are in no wise the children of God; how can we be sharers of the divine nature if God does not dwell within us?"[6]

The theologians also attest to the unity of grace and the divine indwelling. Suarez says: "When God pours out in the soul, the gifts of sanctifying grace, it is not only these gifts, but the Divine Persons themselves who enter the soul and begin to dwell there..."[7]

The doctrine of the teaching Church also makes it abundantly clear that this new presence of the Spirit is reserved to the just. In all creatures God is present by his Immensity, as cause of their being, but in the just the Divinity becomes present in a new way. The Holy Spirit is said to be moving the sinner to penance but not yet to inhabit the sinner. Thus the Council of Trent, speaking of attrition, based on motives that include the fear of hell and certainly do not exclude dead faith, declares this attrition to be a gift of the Holy Spirit, "not yet inhabiting but only moving" the soul[8]. This text certainly seems to suggest that the absence of grace is incompatible with the presence of the divine inhabitation.

Again in condemning the errors of Baius, the Church teaches that there is no indwelling granted to the sinner. "Moreover that distinction of a twofold justice, one which is brought to pass through the indwelling Spirit of Charity, the other which arises from the inspiration of the Holy Spirit exciting the heart to penance, but not yet dwelling in the heart and diffusing charity in it, by which the justification of the divine law may be fulfilled, is similarly condemned."[9] From this text, it might be reasonably deduced that the sinner who has gravely offended God does not possess the new presence of the Spirit that we call the indwelling or inhabitation. He is indeed moved and aided by actual graces, solicited to penance by them, but he does not possess the gift of the indwelling Spirit. The text does not distinguish here between different classes of sinners to teach that some have the Holy Spirit present and indwelling despite their sin, while others do not. It simply declares that the sinner is solicited to penance without enjoying the indwelling. Thus the text does not imply, for example, any privileged state for the sinner who has retained dead faith. It cannot be said to suggest that this sinner at least retains the inhabitation, if others do not. We may reasonably conclude that if the sinner has sinned gravely, whatever be the nature of the sin, he does not possess the gift of the indwelling Spirit. Then too Leo XIII had used expressions which dissuade us from any disassociation of grace and the gift of the divine indwelling. In *Divinum Illud* he says: "... even in those men who lived before Christ, the Holy Spirit dwelled ..." and again "... The beginning of man's rebirth and renewal takes place at Baptism, for in that Sacrament the unclean spirit is driven forth from the soul and, for the first time, the Holy Spirit comes and renders the soul deiform." And in the same document, the Pontiff says, "... Moreover by grace God dwells in the soul as in a temple."[10]

St. Thomas writes: "I answer that the Divine Person is fittingly sent in the sense that He newly exists in anyone; and He is given or possessed by anyone; and neither of these is otherwise than by sanctifying grace.

"For God is in all things by his essence, power, and presence, according to his common mode, as the cause existing in the effects which participate in his goodness. Above and beyond this common mode, however, there is one special mode belonging to the rational nature wherein God is said to be present as the object known is in the knower, and the beloved in the lover. And since the rational creature by its operation of knowledge and love attains to God himself, according to this special mode God is said not only to exist in the rational creature but also to dwell therein as in his own temple. So no other effect can be put down as the reason why the Divine Person is in the rational creature in a new mode, except sanctifying grace. Hence the Divine Person is sent, and proceeds temporally, only according to sanctifying grace.

"Again we are said to possess only what we can freely use and enjoy; and to have the power of enjoying the Divine Person can only be according to sanctifying grace. And yet the Holy Spirit is possessed by man, and dwells within him, in the very gift of sanctifying grace. Hence the Holy Spirit himself is given and sent."[11]

From the doctrine of revelation then we can conclude that there is a presence of God reserved exclusively to the just. We see that this presence is not merely moral, in the sense that it could be had by any man, including a sinner, who set his mind to think of God. The sources of revelation speak of a new ontological presence of God, of the

Spirit, of the Trinity. They speak of the substance of the Divinity inhabiting the just, of the Trinity that takes up its abode in the just soul. This implies that the just soul truly has the divine substance present to it in some way, in some new way.

It is important to observe that while the sources quoted above mention justice as a condition for this new presence, nowhere do they imply that a high degree of sanctity or mystical experience is a necessary precondition to this presence. On the contrary the fact that this presence comes with Baptism shows clearly enough that what is required is the state of grace as such and not some particularly elevated degree of grace or of the mystical life. "... The beginning of man's rebirth and renewal takes place at Baptism, for in that sacrament the unclean spirit is driven forth from the soul and, for the first time, the Holy Spirit comes and renders the soul deiform."[12] No theory that endangers this truth can be accepted to explain the doctrine of the divine indwelling. Aphraates, one of the early Fathers of the Church, declares: "At Baptism we have received the spirit of Christ. At the very moment when the priest invokes the Holy Spirit, heaven opens and he descends, broods over the waters and dwells in those who are baptized. For the Holy Spirit is absent from all those born of the body until they come to this fountain of regeneration. Then they receive the Holy Spirit."[13] This passage expresses the faith of the early Church, underscoring the facts of the divine inhabitation. Before Baptism man has not the Holy Spirit. At Baptism the soul receives the Holy Spirit. No further condition is mentioned. There is no suggestion that an advanced spiritual life is necessary. We also cannot suppose that any such condition is presupposed for the reception of the Sacrament. He who is baptized receives the Holy Spirit. So new is this presence that he who lacks it is said simply not to possess the Holy Spirit. "The fountainhead of all these gifts is Baptism. At Baptism we receive the remission of our sins, sanctification, a share in the life of the Spirit, divine adoption and eternal life."[14]

The Holy Spirit who comes as an abiding Guest remains with the justified soul as long as the soul does not grievously offend God. "When a man falls away from God by sin, grace will be restored if he repents. But sinful man is no longer in God, since the Holy Spirit, who is in God, has departed from him."[15]

There is evident in the writings of the early Church an especial assimilation of Penance to the sacrament of Baptism, in that both confer the Holy Spirit. Nowhere do we find any other conditions mentioned than the conditions necessary for the fruitful, valid reception of the sacrament. There is no question of the necessity of subsequent acts of the penitent required to supply for the insufficiency of Penance or Baptism in conferring the Holy Spirit. Nowhere do we find the presence of the Holy Spirit attached to the condition of a mystical life. The sacrament justifies, gives grace and the new presence of the Holy Spirit. St. Cyprian teaches that those who repent and receive "peace" receive also the Holy Spirit. In fact he himself grants "peace" to them even before the ordinary space of penance is completed in order that they may face imminent persecution "possessing the Holy Spirit".[16] Even a low level of spiritual life, provided grace is present, seems to be sufficient to grant the Christian the divine indwelling. There is no suggestion that even the reconciled apostates had to wait a long development of their mystical life before the divine inhabitation was achieved. They repented; they received the peace; they possessed the Holy Spirit.

St. Ambrose speaks of the reconciled sinner as being signed with the Holy Spirit.[17]

Again we see that the mere state of grace gives the divine inhabitation. The lowest level of divine life seems to be compatible with the divine indwelling. No further conditions are mentioned or implied as necessary.

St. Jerome remarks that the priest who imposes his hands on the sinner to be reconciled with the Church "invokes the return of the Holy Spirit."[18] It is unquestionably the teaching of the sources of revelation that with the advent of grace in Baptism or Penance the Holy Spirit is given ad indwelling. One cannot therefore construct a theory that postpones this new presence until the baptized has achieved certain acts, nor until he has attained to a certain degree of experimental intimacy with God. There is a divine inhabitation. It is given with justice. It differs so from the mere presence of immensity that when the presence of immensity alone is had the Holy Spirit is said to be absent. The data of revelation proclaim these facts as certain. A theologian can obviously not limit the presence of the Holy Spirit beyond the limits suggested by revelation. A contrite sinner may have prepared himself to receive grace through attrition and approach to the sacrament of penance. He may have to his credit no act of perfect charity, but he has fulfilled the essential conditions to receive grace, and with grace he will possess the indwelling Spirit. The baptized infant prior to any act, be it of faith or charity, possesses the same indwelling Spirit. The divine indwelling cannot be made to depend upon the actual exercise of an act of faith or charity. This would be contrary to the clear teaching of the Church.

Any theory concerning the nature of the divine indwelling must so explain the indwelling that the baptized child or the adult is assured of the new presence. Since, moreover, the sources of revelation show us the indwelling as already realized with the state of grace one must avoid any explanation which would reduce the presence of the Spirit to a mere potential presence in the soul of the baptized, a presence that will become actual only when further conditions are realized. This is true whether these conditions are to be realized only in heaven, as, for example, the condition of the light of glory, or whether these conditions are to be fulfilled by the soul on this earth, but are unrealizable at the moment of Baptism, or the infusion of grace, as, for example, a mystical experience of God, an experimental knowledge of God, or the positing of actual acts of knowledge and love of God. For revelation by no means indicates that what is given to the baptized child or the attrite sinner who receives the sacrament of Penance without perfect contrition is merely a virtual presence of God, or a merely potential presence of God to become actual later. No. The most superficial study of the Fathers and of the teaching of the Church indicates that the baptized child and the repentant sinner possess God actually present in a new way, have already in essence the indwelling of the divine substance. To declare this presence merely virtual or potential would be to go directly contrary to revealed truth. Given grace we have the divine indwelling, and my explanation of how this indwelling takes place must cover this fact.

What we have seen so far in our brief study of the data of revelation indicates then that there is a presence of God reserved to the just. This presence is not merely a mental presence, but the presence of the very substance of the Trinity. This new presence is given at Baptism or at the moment when grace returns to the sinner's soul.

Besides the created gift of grace that comes to the soul with justification, there is another gift, the Uncreated Gift. In justification God himself is given, passes over somehow into the possession of the just man. For in the justified man, God, the divine substance, comes to dwell, to "inhabit". He is spoken of by revelation as being present in a new way to souls in the state of grace. He is not so present to those in grave sin. Since the presence of immensity is common to all created reality, we can conclude that the presence of God in the just soul is not merely the presence of immensity. This latter presence is required by all creatures simply in order to be at all, to continue in being, and to operate according to their respective natures.

In justification the divine substance is "given" to the justified soul. That is what revelation tells us. It speaks clearly of a giving. By giving is meant in ordinary speech the gratuitous handing over of something from the possession of the giver to the possession of him who receives. The process of justification somehow involves a giving which terminates in the true possession of the Divinity by the just soul. This is merely an analysis of the term "gift" applied by revelation to the Holy Spirit. If then the Holy Spirit by appropriation, or the Trinity is given to the just soul in a new way, it is clearly present to that soul in a new way, a way that was not had before justification. Before justification God was present by power, essence and immensity as he is present to all created being. If the presence we are to explain is a new presence had only by the just, it is more than the presence of immensity.

This new presence is also characterized by at least a relative permanence, for revelation speaks of a dwelling, a making of one's home, a taking up of one's abode.

Some new union of the soul with the Divinity must take place when the soul is justified, if God becomes newly present to it. This union, we have seen, cannot be a mere moral union, a union that is merely psychological or resultant exclusively from our acts of thought and will. The very substance of the Divinity is brought newly present to man in the divine indwelling, and the acts of thought and will are not sufficient to effect this change in man. The soul of the just man is ontologically related to God in a new way. Created grace, inhering in the soul, would appear to be the basis of this new relation. Obviously there can be no change in God when this new relation of presence is set up. The relation is, from God's part, what philosophers call a relation of reason. This means that no new relation comes to be in God, as a real modification of his being. The new modification exists in the creature, on the basis of which we can logically speak of a new relationship between God and the creature, although a change takes place only in the creature, and not in God, when this new relationship is brought into being.

If the foundation of the relation is the absolute perfection of grace it will be inseparably connected with the Uncreated Gift since one does not separate the foundation of a relation and its term.

The presence that revelation speaks of is a substantial presence, a presence of the substantial reality of the Divinity. It is also a new presence of that Substance. It is not merely the presence of immensity. The presence is a physical one, however. It is not merely moral or psychological in the sense that it is produced as an object of thought or of an act of will. Even the sinner or the man possessing dead faith could have that sort of presence. This new presence, however, is had only by those in the state of sanctifying grace.

Revelation makes consistent mention also of a created gift of grace in connection with the divine indwelling, a created gift which is distinct from the uncreated gift of the Holy Spirit.[19] Since this gift of sanctifying grace is superadded to a fully constituted human nature, to the complete substance of a man, it can only have the nature of what scholastic philosophers call an accident. An accident is a being or reality which does not exist in itself. It exists as a qualification or modification of a being. It inheres in this being. A man is a substance, existing in himself. His characteristic qualities, capacities, activities, size and shape are accidents. They inhere in him as qualifications or further modifications of his substantial being. Grace is a reality which inheres in the soul. It is capable of growth. It is then an absolute accident.[20] It is a positive entity, in other words, but an accidental one, and not a substance. It is a supernatural accident, however, and not a natural one. Grace appears to be a created, spiritual, supernatural, absolute, qualitative accident. It inheres in the soul. It empowers the soul to produce supernatural acts, acts that bear a proportion to a supernatural end. With grace, the soul is constituted a radical principle for the production of acts that lead to the attainment of God as God is in himself. By grace man is constituted a sharer in the divine nature. He is made just intrinsically. Finally, it should be mentioned again that there is a fundamental connection between the presence of sanctifying grace and the presence of the indwelling Spirit. The divine indwelling cannot be spoken of as having taken place except on the condition of the presence of sanctifying grace in the soul. But which comes first, sanctifying grace or the divine indwelling? In the order of time, it seems obvious that neither precedes the other. They occur simultaneously. In the order of being, however, which has the primacy? Does sanctifying grace bring the divine indwelling, or is it the other way around? And what is the precise nature of the link between grace and the divine inhabitation? These are some of the questions which any theory of the nature or mode of the divine indwelling must attempt to answer.

NOTES

[1] Iraeneus, *Demonstrationes Praedicationis Apostolicae*, Smith, (A.C.W. 16), p. 51, Newman Press, Md. 1952.

[2] *P.G.* 5, 652.

[3] *Ibid.*

[4] *Adversus Graecos,* 13, *P.G.* 6, 835.

[5] *Ep. 187 ad Dardanum*, Caput V, P.L. 33, 237-838.

[6] *In Joannem*, 9, *P.G.* 74, 260.

[7] 12 B, c. 5, n. 8.

[8] Denzinger 898.

[9] Denzinger 1063.

[10] A.S.S., XXIX, 645-647.

[11] *S.T.*, I, q. 43, a. 3, c.

[12] A.S.S., XXXIX, 546-647; 652.

[13] *Demonstrationes*, 6, 14, P.S. I, 291.

[14] St. John Chrysostom, *In Actus Apostolorum*, 40, 2; P.G. 60, 285.

[15] St. Athanasius, *Adversus Arianos*, IV, 3, 24; P.G. 26, 375.

[16] *Epist.* LVII, 4; CV 3, 653.

[17] *De Poenitentia*, II, 3, 18; P.L. 16, 522.

[18] *Dial. cont. Lucifer*, 8; P.L. 23, 167.

[19] Denzinger 799.

[20] Denzinger 800-803.

Chapter 2. Revelation and the
Divine Indwelling

REVELATION speaks not only of a new presence but also of a new possession of God by the just soul. Since the only way a spirit can be possessed is by acts of love and knowledge, it is evident that with justification comes some new capacity to know and to love God. The just soul is indeed capable of enjoying the divine Guest. The divine indwelling cannot be explained as a dead presence, an inert gift, however new and important that Gift might be. Rather it implies the taking possession of that gift, the use and enjoyment of that gift. It implies a spiritual exchange between the persons involved. It will result in a profound joy to the just soul who lays hold of and enjoys the divine Guest.

By intellect and will the soul can now be united to the divine Guest, can enjoy his presence. There will be made possible a reciprocal exchange of thoughts, affections, desires. Friendship, with all that it implies, can be said to flourish between the just soul and its Guest. A union of thought and of will is possible between the soul and God. It might appear to be appropriate to call this union a subjective union, but it is generally referred to as an objective union by reason of the fact that in this union the just soul consciously possesses God as its object. The objective union of thought and will is thus able to be contrasted with the ontological union between the soul and God that is brought about by the new presence of God to the soul in the state of sanctifying grace. The objective union here in question is based upon this new presence and its resultant ontological union. This objective union is of paramount importance and no explanation of the divine indwelling that does not account for it can be an adequate explanation. Presence is not the only element that tradition shows us in the divine indwelling. There is also a new radical capacity to possess God. There is the new capacity for what is called an objective union.

A profound union of faith and charity results from justification, a sweet familiarity, an affectionate intimacy. The soul is brought into a new unity with God, a loving unity, a unity of heart and mind. This loving unity is an essential element in the divine inhabitation as it is described by the sources of revelation. A new presence must be accounted for and a new objective unity.

According to revelation, God does not become newly present to the just soul there to remain inert and inoperative. He stimulates a constant exchange of affections and thoughts between himself and the soul he has honored with his presence. He draws the soul to an ever deeper objective union. A moral union of the highest order can be the complete flowering of the original gift. The soul is now equipped with a superior capacity to know and love God in a way that surpasses all its natural faculties and bears a proportion to a strictly supernatural end, to God as he is in himself and not only as he is seen in his participated perfections. In the normal course of this life the devout soul will actualize this new power of knowledge and love in varying degrees. To the gift of presence is added the new power to possess God in an incomparably superior way and an invitation to a hitherto impossible intimacy with the Creator. The soul may truly be said to have God, to possess God, to enjoy God. Thus the presence of the divine inhabitation has quite another character than the ordinary presence of immensity. The hidden God of immensity now gives himself over to the delightful possession of the creature. He may truly be said to pass into the possession of his creature whom he has elevated to this power of possession. He not only deifies us by his presence, he not only renders us like to him but he renders us such sharers of his nature that we can know him as he knows himself. We possess heaven already in germ. Grace and the accompanying virtues, while they are distinct from the acts that proceed from them are nonetheless entirely ordered to these acts of knowledge and love. The Divine Persons who implant these virtues of faith and hope and charity within the soul, implant them there that the soul may activate them and possess the divine Giver thereof.

The just soul, raised to a superior level of life, is called upon to imitate the intellectuality of the Trinity, to share in the life of the Trinity, to know God as he knows himself and to love God as he loves himself. The very purpose of the Trinity's indwelling is to associate the soul to the happiness of the Triune life. It is only to the graced soul that God so delivers himself over. He is elsewhere, but he is not possessed elsewhere. This intimacy of love, this sharing of friendship, this communication of divine goods, is not had when God is present only by immensity. Sacred Scripture underscores this note of peculiarly friendly presence when it refers to the soul as the "temple" of the Holy Spirit.

The Trinity is present to the just soul not as to a dead temple but as to a living temple, a temple which is a living soul capable of being raised above the level of the natural condition of servant to the condition of adopted child. A share in that divine life of the Trinity is now accorded to the soul. The soul is introduced into the intimate life of the Trinity. It is united to God whom it may possess at will by acts of charity and faith. The soul now has always within reach this power to know and love God. It can actualize this power and it can grow constantly in its union with the God newly present to it. God solicits the soul to do just that.

When God thus takes up his residence in the soul, he deploys his treasures there, he acts upon the soul, elevating its faculties, granting to the soul the new powers necessary to enjoy at will the divine Guest. The very purpose of this new presence is to orientate the soul and empower it to use these faculties of possession. The Divine Persons give themselves to the soul that the soul may be able to receive Them, to possess Them, to enjoy Them. They plant in the soul the faculties which will flower into eternal life, which assure to the soul on earth a new possession of the Trinity and which are the means to an eternity of companionship with the celestial court. For the space of the earthly pilgrimage the Beatific Vision is withheld, but already the soul possesses the remote principle of that vision. Already a new possession is had, infinitely superior to any "possession" that could be spoken of in connection with God's presence of immensity. The operations of the just soul now terminate in the God who has made these operations possible by his grace. If acts of faith and love are not indispensable conditions for the coming of the Trinity to the soul for the first time they are nevertheless the means by which the soul exercises its vital possession of the God already present. The soul in grace possesses the faculties really to enjoy the divine Guest. The actual exercise of these acts of possession may be dependent upon various extrinsic factors. The faculties themselves are already given. There is then present in the baptized infant an actual presence which is new and a virtual possession which is new also and which waits only upon the development of knowledge and will to become actual. The Trinity came to the soul to accomplish a work of love. Their presence in the soul is no cold and inert presence. They have given themselves to us as a gift to be really possessed through the new faculties of possession with which they have instructed the soul.

The state of grace alone suffices to assure then a very real possession of God. The developments of the future, the active and passive union of prayer, the mystical states, the ineffable vision reserved for heaven—all these will be developments within that same divine order to which God elevated the soul at justification. Present by grace, possessed by the just soul, the Trinity invites the soul to the full deployment of the divine energies it has planted in the soul with Its coming. The Trinity has come to the soul with this transforming aim; that the soul might taste and see that the Lord is sweet. A new presence and a new possession have both been accomplished and both must be accounted for in our attempt to offer a theoretical elucidation of the divine indwelling.

The note of possession is given to us clearly in those passages of Holy Scripture which speak of the Holy Spirit as a Gift. St. Thomas too observes concerning possession, and the notion of presence, that the divine inhabitation implies more than a certain type of new relation. The soul must possess God in some fashion.[1]

An analysis of the minimal concept of gift reveals a number of obvious facts. When a gift is given there is a giver and a recipient.

There is a movement of liberality or love at the source of the gift. There is a passing over of something into the real possession of the receiver, so that he may truly be said to possess it, to have it, to use and enjoy it at his discretion.

The possession of God by the just soul is repeatedly underscored by St. Paul in his epistles. In verse five of chapter five of the Epistle to the Romans we read: "and hope does not disappoint us, because God's love has been poured into our hearts through the Holy Spirit who has been given to us." In chapter eight, verse nine, of the same epistle, St. Paul identifies appurtenance to Christ and the possession of his Spirit: "But you are not in the flesh, you are in the Spirit, if the Spirit of God really dwells in you. Anyone who does not have the Spirit of Christ does not belong to him." In the first Epistle to the Corinthians, St. Paul declares that he has received the Spirit of God. The Christians also possess the Spirit as in a temple (I Cor. 6, 19). They are temples of "the Holy Spirit within you, which you have from God." God has given to us the pledges, the first fruits of the Spirit (2 Cor. 5,5). By the Christian's faith in Christ, he has received the Spirit (Gal. 3,2). To the sons of God, God has sent His Spirit to inspire the spirit of worship in them (Gal. 4,6). God the Father has given His Holy Spirit to be in us (I Thess. 4,8). We are renewed in the Spirit whom God has poured out on us richly through Jesus Christ (Tit. 3,5).

St. John stresses this relationship of union when he tells us that he who loves is born of God and knows God; again that if we love one another God will abide with us. God is love and who abides in love abides in God and God abides in him (I Jn. 4,8; 4,12; 4,16).

The Fathers of the Church also have set forth this privilege of possession that God grants to the just soul. St. Cyril of Alexandria says that without this possession of the Holy Spirit there is no question of our being truly children of God.[2] Novatian describes the Spirit as given to us as the architect of our spiritual life.[3] We have received him in baptism and he regenerates us in that sacrament, says Aphraates.[4] He is granted to all who confess Christ, says St. Athanasius.[5] It is because we possess the Spirit that we also possess the entire Trinity, Chryostom tells us.[6] We merit to be called gods for we possess God dwelling within us permanently, adds St. Cyril of Alexandria.[7] And because we have received the Spirit we share in the life of God. St. Gregory expresses the intimate union that results from grace with beauty: God is united to gods and is intimately known by them, he tells us.[8] In the Homily of the Gospel of Pentecost St. Augustine reminds his Christians that although the world cannot know the Holy Spirit, the just man can for he dwells within the just.

We are then given a true possession of the Holy Spirit, of the substance of the Divinity, such a possession as can exist between persons, a spiritual possession of knowledge and love.

These two central facts, the facts of the ontological presence of the very substance of the Trinity and psychological possession of the Trinity within, present us with the theological problem connected with the divine indwelling. The divine inhabitation must so be explained as not to prejudice these two truths: a substantial presence and a true possession, and both accomplished somehow at the moment of justification. The soul, before any act, has God substantially present. The soul, by its acts, is able to take possession of, to enjoy the divine Guest so present. These are the two most important elements in our problem with which revelation presents us. We must reconcile an ontological union with a psychological possession, a presence had before the possibility of any act, and a union through a possession that is new with grace.

God is not only newly present. He is also possessed by our acts of knowledge and love. He is also newly present before these acts are possible.

Leo XIII strongly emphasizes this new possession of God, this objective union that follows upon God's presence: "The beginning of man's rebirth and renewal takes place at baptism, for in that sacrament the unclean spirit is driven forth from the soul, and for the first time the Holy Spirit comes and renders the soul deiform . . . He exists in man not only as he does in inanimate things but more so in that he is known and loved. . . . Wherefore through grace he dwells in the just as in a temple in a wholly singular and intimate fashion. Hence too there follows that need for charity, by which the soul clings to God most closely, more closely than a friend to his most precious friend, and enjoys his presence fully and sweetly. This marvellous union, moreover, which is called the inhabitation differs only in condition or state from the beatific union of the blessed . . ."[9]

This passage reiterates several points we have already seen concerning the divine indwelling. This indwelling or inhabitation takes place at the moment of justification, not therefore as the result of acts following upon justification. It involves moreover a presence different from the presence of immensity. It implies a loving union of affections and knowledge, a union by which the soul enjoys God truly present. And this union differs only in condition or state from that of heaven.

This document of Leo XIII has at times been interpreted as favoring a purely objective theory of the divine indwelling. How false such an interpretation is, is clear from the Pontiff's statement that it is the sacrament of baptism that brings the Holy Spirit to inhabit the soul. The sacrament of baptism is not normally conferred after acts of faith and charity on the part of the infant. A new presence and a new radical power to possess are stressed in this document, but there is not the slightest suggestion of anything favoring a theory of an exclusively objective union. On the contrary such a theory is openly excluded unless it satisfactorily explains the presence of God in the infant soul prior to any acts.

The encyclical on the mystical body, of Pius XII, repeats these two elements in describing the divine indwelling. Since this document also has been considered by some to teach an exclusively objective union, let us see what it has to say.

"Indeed, the Divine Persons are said to indwell inasmuch as being present in an inscrutable manner in animate creatures endowed with intellect they are attained by them through knowledge and love, yet in an intimate and unique manner that transcends all nature."[10]

Thus presence and possession are again enumerated but it is undeniably clear here that the new and mysterious presence is not due to acts, but that rather these acts of knowledge and love of the God so present follow upon this presence. "Present in an inscrutable manner", these Persons are attained by knowledge and love. The mysterious presence of the divine inhabitation certainly seems to precede the possession by acts of knowledge and love. But the attainment of the Divine

Persons by a transcendent knowledge and love is equally emphasized as a privilege of the new state.

Thus revelation has presented to us in clear general terms the outline of our problem, which is, to explain the mode of the divine indwelling. It has set forth the problem and its limits. Has it given us further hints as to the path of its solution? It has, at least negatively. For we have this much from revelation: no theory that explains the divine inhabitation merely on the basis of ordinary creative causal activity will suffice. That would give us merely a higher degree of participation, not a specifically new presence. And the presence of the indwelling is now, reserved to the just. No theory that would explain this new presence as a psychological presence, a merely moral presence can be correct for revelation teaches that God becomes present and not that the *idea* of God becomes present. No theory that explains the new presence as a result of actual acts can be correct for the divine indwelling takes place, beyond any doubt, at *justification* and acts are not possible to the infant. Obviously also no theory that compromises the difference between Creator and creature can be acceptable for the divine inhabitation does not destroy these essential differences. Nor can we so explain the indwelling as to contradict the truth that all God's actions outside the Trinity are common to all three persons of the Trinity.

Beyond these general outlines of the problem, can we find in revelation indications of the more intimate nature of the mode of the divine indwelling? .A careful study of the data of revelation leads to the conviction that in some way God acts toward the soul in the manner of what philosophers call a formal cause. Revelation suggests that formal causality of some type, extrinsic and exemplary, or intrinsic, quasi-formal, plays a role in the divine inhabitation. It sanctions the theological attempts which have been made to understand the divine indwelling in terms of one or another kind of formal causality.

NOTES

[1] *In Sent.*, dist. 14, q. 2, a. 2, ad 2.
[2] *In Joan.; P.G.* 74, 545.
[3] *De Trin.*, 29; *P.L.* 3, 973.
[4] *Demonstrationes*, 6, 14; *P.S.* 1, 291.

5 *Adversus Arianos*, 3, 24; *P.G.* 26, 373.
6 *In Epist. ad Rom. Homilia* 13, 8; *P.G.* 60, 519.
7 *In Joannem Comm.*, I, 9; 14, 17; *P.G.* 73, 128 et 74, 260.
8 *Orat.* 38, n. 7; *P.G.* 36, 317.
9 *Divinum Illud*, A.S.S., 29, 652-653.
10 A.S.S., 35, 231-232.

Chapter 3.　Formal Causality and the Greek Fathers

THE indwelling of God in the soul of the just man is a mystery. We cannot hope to understand it completely and with perfect clarity. Revelation is not precise and explicit about the mode of the Trinity's inhabitation of the soul in grace. Theologians have developed different theories to explain it. No single theory has won the unanimous approval of the theologians. All agree, however, that the problem of the divine indwelling has to be discussed in terms of causality. The presence of God to creatures becomes intelligible through the various forms of causality he can be appreciated as exerting on them.

Philosophers distinguish different types of causality. Every one of these types may be involved, each in its own way, in the entire production of a single effect. We must never forget, moreover, that any type of causality which is attributed to God has to be predicted of him in an analogical way. This is particularly important to remember in the case of the formal causality which we shall speak about in connection with the doctrine of the divine indwelling.

The kind of causality that generally comes to mind first when we think of two things which are related as cause and effect is *efficient causality*. An efficient cause is responsible for an effect through its action. Thus a painter produces a painting by his action with paint and brush, and God produces creatures and sustains them in being by the action of his creative will. Both of these are instances of efficient causality, the one on the level of the creature, the other on the level of the Creator. God's presence of immensity, his presence to all beings as their creator and conserver, involves his efficient causality.

Another type of causality is final causality. A final cause does not perform any action. It is responsible for an effect as being the end or purpose which attracts and motivates an efficient cause to act and so produce the desired effect. The effect occurs because of the action of the efficient cause. The action of the efficient cause, however, and therefore its effect, occurs only because of the influence of the final cause.

Still another form of causality is material causality. A material cause, unlike an efficient or a final cause, both of which are extrinsic, is intrinsic to an effect. A material cause functions as a constitutive principle of the very essence of an effect. It is, so to speak, the underlying subject in the basic structure of an effect. It is in potency to a form. Receiving the form, its potency is actualized. It is in act with respect to the form. The form perfects it. As it receives the form, however, the form is simultaneously contracted and individuated by the material cause. The subject and its form—better perhaps, the "informed" subject—thus constitute the complete essence of the effect. The effect is composed of matter, a principle of potency and limitation, and form, a principle of act and perfection. In a marble statue, for example, the marble is the material cause of the statue. The statue exists as an effect because the marble is present and has received the form of a statue. The form actualizes the marble to be a statue in act rather than in mere potency. But as the form of a statue is received in the marble, it is contracted and individuated within the limits of the marble.

A final type of causality to be considered is the one known as formal causality. A formal cause is responsible in its own way for the specific character or actual perfection of the nature of an effect. It functions as a cause by being that whose specific perfection is communicated to the effect, so that the effect can be said actually to share in that perfection. The specific nature of the effect somehow derives from the presence of that whose perfection is being communicated to and shared in by the effect.

If an effect is brought about in imitation of something else, so that the specific character of the effect derives from the fact that it is an image of something else, the reality so imitated can be considered a formal cause. The effect possesses its own perfection only because it is an image of the perfection originally contained in the other reality. It shares in the other's perfection because it is imaging that perfection. The formal perfection of the other reality makes possible its being reflected or imitated in the effect. In this sense, the other reality is a cause of the specific character of the effect. The other reality, however, is not a constitutive principle, intrinsic to the being of the effect itself. It is therefore an extrinsic cause. Extrinsic formal causality is more commonly referred to as exemplary causality.

Formal causality in the strict sense is, like material causality, intrinsic to the effect. A formal cause functions as a constitutive principle of the very essence of an effect. It involves the communication of a form to matter. The matter is actualized, perfected, given a specific character by the form. Thus marble has to receive a form in order to be actualized, perfected as, and given the specific character of a statue. The perfection of the form is present and communicated to the matter. The specific character of the marble as a statue derives from the presence of the form in whose perfection the marble shares as it is communicated to it. The statue itself is constituted by the union of the marble and the form communicated to it.

The example we have used illustrates formal causality on the accidental level. All accidents are forms. They are communicated to matter which is already constituted as a certain kind of matter on the substantial level by an appropriate substantial form. In the case of man, for example, matter has been rendered a human body by the presence of the soul as the substantial form which actuates and specifies matter on the substantial level as a human body rather than as some other kind of body. It is the union of these two principles, matter and the soul, that constitutes the one complete substance of man, whose specific character as a human being derives from the fact that his soul is the substantial form of his body.

A number of important theologians have argued that revelation suggests some type of formal causality as playing a role in the divine indwelling. What is the scriptural and patristic basis for attempting an explanation by formal causality?

There are certain texts of St. Paul which could be reasonably construed to suggest formal causality. These are the texts in which the Holy Spirit is spoken of as sealing and anointing the grace-informed soul. The comments of the Greek Fathers on these texts are what has given rise to the question of the possibility of seeking in formal causality an explanation of the mode of the divine indwelling. There has been a tendency in modern theology to contrast the so-called oriental theology on this matter with Latin theology. These two views are seen as complementary rather than contradictory.

Before we deal with the relevant texts of St. Paul it may be well to inquire into the general Pauline concept of justification. Justification, according to St. Paul, entails a mystical identification with Christ. Baptism signifies the death of the old man and a rebirth of the new man in Christ. The Christian becomes identified mystically with the death and resurrection of Christ. He is a member of Christ's mystical body.

The man reborn in Christ is also spoken of as enjoying a certain life "in the Spirit". The just man is said to possess the Spirit of Christ. Because he possesses the Spirit of Christ, the just man enjoys a life "in the spirit". The just man is distinguished by the possession of "spirit". This "spirit" appears to be viewed as transforming, internally renewing and sanctifying a man. It would seem to be an inherent quality of the soul. Theologians call it created sanctifying grace.

What is the relation between the created gift and the Holy Spirit, between the "spirit" (pneuma) and the "Spirit" (Pneuma)? St. Paul seems to insinuate that there exists a very definite relation between the two. He seems to insinuate that "spirit" owes its existence to the presence of "Spirit".

In Romans 8,9, for example, "to be in the Spirit" seems to follow upon possession of the Spirit of Christ. The analogy of the seal in Ephesians 1,13 might be seen again as suggesting that a man's "being sealed" is due to the action of the Seal. The inherent "sealing" is accomplished by the Holy Spirit as the Seal. Thus the entire concept of justification in St. Paul might be construed as having a certain unity in that the central concept is that of the Gift of the Holy Spirit, and the other significations of spirit, such as the created gift, would be secondary and derived. All spiritual treasures would be an effect of this possession of the Uncreated Spirit. The interior sanctification of man is primarily a communication of the Personal Spirit of God. All "spiritual existence" appears as a consequence, as an effect of the possession of the Uncreated Grace.

St. Paul seems to insinuate that created grace is caused in the soul through the very communication, the sharing in, the reception of the Holy Spirit. If this be true, is there not here a suggestion that created grace is produced not by a causality that is exclusively efficient causality, on the part of God? Karl Rahner suggests that at least from the structure of his concept of Pneuma, we could say that, according to St. Paul, since we have the personal Spirit of God, we also possess our spiritual being (esse pneumatikos), our created sanctifying grace.[1] For the more scholastic expression "because we have grace, we have the Holy Spirit", however, we do not find in St. Paul so immediate and clear a formulation.

Most of those theologians who would establish the theory of formal causality in the divine inhabitation lean more heavily upon the Greek Fathers than upon St. Paul. Karl Rahner is of the opinion that the Fathers, at least the Greek Fathers, show us created grace as the consequence of the substantial participation of the Uncreated Gift.[2] P. Dumont considers that in opting for the anteriority of the divine inhabitation over the supernatural virtues, one would have the advantage of conforming more to the manner in which the Fathers habitually speak of grace.[3]

There are many authorities who believe that the Greek Fathers suggest a priority of nature on the part of the Uncreated Gift and some type of formal causality on the part of the Holy Spirit in the production of grace.[4] These authorities would read the Greek Fathers, when they speak of a deification of man that takes place by a sharing of the Divinity, as holding that the new image of God that comes to the soul is the result of this communication of the Spirit to the soul. We become "sharers in the divine nature" by this new image of God, a created image which results from the immediate application of the Holy Spirit to the substance of the soul. It is indisputable that the Fathers insist strongly upon the point that no creature as such can divinize the soul. On the contrary.

The Holy Spirit (or at times the Eternal Word) himself is said to deify us immediately.

St. Cyril of Alexandria says: "The Holy Spirit works directly in us by uniting us to himself, joining our souls to his Being, so that we may become sharers in the divine nature."[5] The same point is being made when he declares: "...it would be absurd to ascribe to a creature the action by which we are made sharers of the divine nature. For no creature can communicate to another that which is above the creaturely."[6] And again: "The Spirit is God, who deifies us, not through the ministry of grace alone, but by pouring himself out upon the just, making them to share the divine nature."[7] It appears also that the new image of God, the created image, arises from this communication of the Spirit to the soul as a consequence of the transferring effect of the Spirit. "For Christ is formed in us when the Holy Spirit pours into us a divine form at justification. Thus it is that the character of the substance of God and of the Father shines up in our souls."[8]

The activity of the Holy Spirit is to transform the soul somehow into himself, divinizing it. He sculpts there the divine features, imprints the divine likeness. "Transforming the souls of men as it were into himself, he sculpts there the image and likeness of the Supreme Substance."[9] A divine character is imprinted in us "through" our sharing in the Holy Spirit. "Through the Holy Spirit, a divine character is imprinted in us; we are remade in the likeness of Christ Jesus as in the likeness of an image ... made sharers in the Holy Spirit."[10]

St. Cyril's doctrine seems to be clear. Far from being a consequence of the presence of grace, the created gift, the presence of the Spirit seems to have a certain priority. The divine character, the new image arises from the presence of the Holy Spirit conferring Himself upon the soul. No created being would be sufficient to deify man. This St. Cyril repeats tirelessly. So much emphasis does he and the other Greek Fathers lay upon this point that from its evidence they prove the divinity of the Holy Spirit and the Eternal Word who do indeed deify us. If the Holy Spirit deifies us, he is divine. If the Eternal Word deifies us he is divine. It would seem that in the mind of the Fathers nothing less than the substance of the Divinity can divinize us. It is by a communication of himself to us that God divinizes us and nothing less than this would suffice. "We are all likewise said to be sharers in the Divine Nature through the Spirit of God. But if the Spirit were a creature then we would most certainly have no share in the Divine Nature, for then we would be joined to a creature and be alien to the Divinity, having no share in his nature. But if we are divinized through the communication of the Holy Spirit, then surely no one would be so absurd as to call the Spirit a creature. It is solely because of His Divinity that those in whom he dwells are called gods."[11]

The same argument is adduced to prove the divinity of the Eternal Word. He is not created, because he deifies us and no created entity can deify us, only the sharing, the participation of the Divinity Itself. St. Athanasius states the argument thus: "By sharing in the nature of the Son, we share in the nature of the Father, since the Son is properly God. If the Son were himself only a created participator and not God and Substantial Image of the Father, then he would not deify others, since he himself would have been deified."[12]

The underlying emphasis here seems to be not that the created gift brings the Holy Spirit present as a consequence, an effect of its own presence, but rather that the Holy Spirit, by his communication of himself to the soul, divinizes it, creates in it a new image of God, renders it a sharer in the divine perfections.

St. Basil denies that the Holy Spirit could be called the source of holiness if he were a creature, for the work of sanctification in his mind is a divine work implying the "communication" of the Spirit himself.[13]

St. Cyril consistently connects very clearly the sanctification or deification of man with the "communication" of the Holy Spirit, in such wise that one might reasonably be led to think that the deification, the new image created, is rather the effect of the communication than something preceding it. "If (the Spirit) were not God nor substantially identical with him, but distinct from God, a creature, then how could we, who are born from him, be said to be born of God? We must either openly confess that the Evangelist lies or, if he be truthful, as is the case, we must admit that the Spirit is God and identical in nature with the Godhead. It is by sharing in his nature ... that we are said to be born of God and hence we are called gods ..."[14]

Thus the Spirit must be divine for he deifies us. No created entity produced by God, would be sufficient to deify us. Certainly this argument on which the Fathers rest the proof for the divinity of the Holy Spirit, strongly emphasizes the role of the Holy Spirit personally in our sanctification. The Divinity Itself and not merely a created entity must somehow be given to the soul, communicated to the soul, before man can be said to be divinized. We are made gods, we are sharers in the divine nature, because we in some way share in the Spirit or in the Eternal Word. "If one denies the Holy Spirit is substantially identical with the Godhead, why should man be deified upon reception of the Holy Spirit? How could we be called temples of God if we receive only a created spirit?"[15]

These citations from the Greek Fathers certainly seem to suggest that the immediate presence and activity of the Divinity is required to sanctify us and that from the communication of the Spirit to the soul there arises the new image of God, the created effect that we call sanctifying grace. A certain priority seems to be granted to the Uncreated Gift over the created.

Those authors who favor an approach to the problem of the divine inhabitation dominated by formal causality have not failed to note the oft-repeated statements of the Fathers concerning the immediate activity of the Holy Spirit in our sanctification and deification. We are, the Fathers note, conformed to the image of God, rendered by the Spirit like to the Son whose Spirit he is. This is achieved by the *immediate* activity of the Divinity upon the soul. We are signed by the Spirit, sealed by the Spirit, anointed by the Spirit, his image is imprinted in us by the Spirit. Moreover the Spirit is not only the artist who paints the image of the Divinity in us but he is also the Image that impresses Itself and so produces a created image in us. He is not merely the sculptor of the seal, he is the Seal Itself. He is not only the giver of the ointment but the Ointment Itself that is poured out in the soul to produce the odor of Christ there. He is the anointing itself. Not only is he the producer of the created image, he seems to produce it by his immediate presence, by his communication, by his self-donation, self-giving, self-conferring.

St. Athanasius remarks that the Holy Spirit is divine for he deifies us and no creature can do that. The doctrine of sigillation or sealing is proposed by St. Athanasius as taught by all and founded upon sacred scripture. The image of God in the soul is the created likeness of the Uncreated Spirit, the Seal, and it arises from the impressing of the Seal upon the soul. The Holy Spirit here seems to be not merely the agent, so to speak, the one impressing the seal, the efficient cause. The role of efficient causality is rather ascribed to the Eternal Word, the Son, in order that the activity of the Spirit as sealing may be underscored. The activity of anointing is the Eternal Word's; the oil is the Spirit. In both images the note of self-communication is strongly suggested.[16]

"The seal bears the image of Christ who seals and those who are sealed are made sharers in his nature. And so those sealed are rightly made sharers in the divine nature, as Peter said."[17] Here again the agent, the one impressing the seal, is distinguished from the Seal that impresses itself upon the soul, and the created image arises from the immediate communication of the Seal, the Spirit, to the soul.

As St. Cyril explains it, the process of deification is as follows: The Spirit is the Image of the Son; he thus renders those in whom he exists "conformed to the Image of the Father, that is, to the Son."[18] The conformity, the new image, arises in us from the presence in us of the Spirit. The suggestion is not found here that the presence of the Spirit is a consequence of the created image.

The following text of St. Cyril is of great interest: "For it is the Spirit who joins and so to speak, unites us to God. When we have received him we are made sharers in the divine nature. We receive him through the Son and in the Son, we receive the Father."[19] Here, as in the other Fathers, the whole Trinity is invoked to explain our deification. He attributes to the presence of the Spirit our sharing of the divine nature and he continues the text by insisting that only the substantial presence of the Divinity can effect such a sharing: "How could we be adopted or made sharers in the divine nature if God does not dwell in us, if we do not adhere to him through our vocation to share in the Spirit?"[20]

The Holy Spirit is represented by St. Cyril as a sculptor who sculpts the Image of the Son on our souls. But it must be noted that, in St. Cyril's image, the Holy Spirit is a sculptor of a very unusual type—for he *transforms the soul somehow into himself,* and thus there results the likeness of the Son. In terms of causality, a person might be excused if he saw here less emphasis on efficient causality than on some type of formal causality. "Union with God can only take place through a participation in the Holy Spirit who communicates to us his proper holiness. The Image of the Father is perfect and the natural Image of the Son is his Spirit. Hence, somehow transforming the souls of men into himself, the Spirit impresses on them a likeness to himself and sculpts in them the likeness of the Supreme Substance."[21]

An even more explicit statement of St. Cyril's position can be found in his *Thessaurus* (Assertio 34): "You are signed with the Holy Spirit of the promise. If you are divinely recreated by the Holy Spirit, how could he be a creature, by whom the image of the divine essence and the seal of the divinity is impressed upon you? For the Holy Spirit does not paint as an ordinary painter, producing in us the image of something other than himself and so conferring upon us a likeness to God. Rather, since he is God, he impresses himself invisibly in the hearts of the just, as a seal in wax, and he restores to men the divine image and produces a likeness to himself, through the communication of himself."

It seems to be clear from this passage that there exists a precedence of the Holy Spirit's presence over that of the image he imprints. Moreover more than efficient causality is suggested. Some type of formal causality seems strongly suggested. The Spirit seems to function as more than an extrinsic agent. He is not only a painter, but "God himself and ... impressed as a seal in wax, paints by a communication of himself."[22]

The power to sanctify belongs exclusively to God, according to St. Cyril. This power he has exercised directly upon the souls of men by granting them a participation, a sharing, a communion with himself, through the communication of the Holy Spirit. "It is otiose to suggest that we are sanctified by a creature, since God in his goodness does not hesitate to approach directly the lowliest of creatures to sanctify them through his Holy Spirit."[23] Here again we hear the note of immediacy. This immediacy comes from "sharing in the Spirit." In Adam the process has been the same: "... the Spirit, who effects a likeness to the divinity itself and who was ineffably impressed as a seal (upon us)."[24]

We have been granted the supreme Gift of the Spirit of God himself who dwells in us personally. "(Christ) has sent to us a heavenly Advocate through whom and in whom he is within us and dwells with us—for he has poured into us One who is not a stranger but his own Spirit, of the same nature as himself and the Father."[25] We are sharers in this Spirit and necessarily so, for "no creature can make us share in what surpasses its own nature."[26] In St. Cyril we find a remarkable insistence upon the sealing of the soul by the Holy Spirit. His attitude, at least at first inspection, could not be said to favor the statement that the Holy Spirit comes to the soul as a consequence of the created gifts. Intent upon proving the divinity of the Holy Spirit, he inquires: "This force which sculpts in us the image of God and which, as a seal, impresses in us the beauty of a lovelier world, is it not the Holy Spirit? Some would have it that he does this not as God but only as the producer of grace within us. Does this mean that grace is sculpted in us but he himself is not impressed? It seems so. But in that case man should not be called an image of God, but rather an image of grace."[27] Again the Spirit, divine in nature, immediately produces grace and produces it not by an extrinsic causality apparently, but by impressing himself as a seal upon the soul.[28]

St. Cyril continues: "If nothing can share in the nature of fire save through fire itself, how can one share in the divine nature, save through God?"[29]

Quotations from St. Cyril could be multiplied almost without end. His doctrine seems sufficiently clear. The Holy Spirit sanctifies us not merely through the medium of a created gift but through the gift of himself, immediately present to the soul in a new way and impressed thereon as a seal. Whence arises the new image of God in the soul: "... The Spirit then is God, who conforms us to God not through the ministry of grace but by conferring himself upon our souls and so making them share in the divine nature."[30]

Evidently the Holy Spirit not only produces grace but produces it in a wholly singular manner, by communicating himself in a fashion which strongly suggests formal causality.

St. Basil also recalls to us this same notion of self-diffusion, self-communication, self-conferring, under the images of fire and light. As we cannot separate the process of heating from the fire, its source, so we cannot separate the process of sanctification from the Holy Spirit, its source. The alteration in the substance that is being heated takes place rather through a communication of a quality by accidental information than by merely efficient causality. St. Basil says: "And as iron which is cast into fire does not lose its own nature as fire but is vehemently enflamed and takes on as it were the nature of fire so that it acts like fire, so, from our sharing with him who is by nature Holy, we become holy."[31] In philosophical terms, we could speak here of an accidental information of the substance of the iron by the fire. The substance of iron and the substance of fire are brought together. Each of them possesses its own substantial form. Somehow, however, the form of fire becomes communicated to the iron, "informs" the iron, so that the iron can be said to possess the form of fire. It does not possess it in a substantial way, however, for then it would have been changed completely from iron into fire. It possesses it in an accidental way, sharing in the perfection of fire, while retaining its own substantial form of iron.

St. Basil pursues the formal causality metaphor still further. As the form in the matter, as the art in the artist, and as a habit in the faculty possessing it, so the Holy Spirit is in the just soul.[32] As health, as heat, or as any healthy quality is in a healthy body, so the Spirit is in the just soul. St. Basil further compares the Spirit to the soul of our souls. As the soul was breathed into Adam's body, so the Spirit is breathed into the just soul.

It is to the credit of the seventeenth-century theologian, Petavius, that he brought to the attention of many theologians the theory of the Greek Fathers on the Holy Spirit. He insisted that they taught a union of substance between the soul and the Holy Spirit, a union involving more than the production of grace by efficient causality. Petavius however did not have the speculative equipment to explain the "how" of such a union. He collated the texts of the Fathers and showed that they emphasized less the efficient causality at work in the production of grace, than grace as an effect of the self-conferring of the Substantial holiness of the Holy Spirit.

Thomassinus, another theologian of the seventeenth century, followed Petavius to some extent, in setting down the thesis that the very substance of the Holy Spirit, Substantial Sanctity, forms and sanctifies the soul in justification. But again there was little more than a reporting of Patristic teaching. The metaphysics of such a position he left to subsequent theologians, who did not in fact seem to be in any great hurry to take up the challenge. The next great name we find associated with the so-called Greek theory of the divine inhabitation is M.J. Scheeben, whose position will be discussed in a subsequent chapter.

Karl Rahner points out that the concept of a priority granted to the Uncreated Gift over the created is not a new one to theologians. It could scarcely be the case after a study of the Fathers.[33] St. Bonaventure and Peter Lombard had stressed the Uncreated Gift, perhaps even over-stressed it to the detriment of created grace. St. Thomas describes the Holy Spirit in one place as an "inherent formal cause" of our sonship. St. Thomas had also noted that the gifts of love and wisdom were produced in our souls by the sigillation of the divine persons.

Leonard Lessius, a great theologian of the sixteenth century, had set forth a similar position on the relation of created gift to Uncreated Gift in The Supreme Good. He enumerates the various types of union between man and God that are possible. The union of sanctifying grace is destined to make of man a son of God. This grace does, not by its own physical perfection, but by acting as a foundation which links man to the Holy Spirit, who confers the divine sonship.[34] In The Divine Perfections Lessius restated his position according to which grace was not the full formal cause of the divine adoption and reserved this privilege to the Holy Spirit who confers adoption by his immediate presence.[35] It is true that Lessius corrected his position after he had been attacked by Ripalda, but in the later, posthumous edition of The Divine Perfections grace is still a disposition to the Uncreated Gift.

Concerning the doctrine of the Greek Fathers, however, we must pay special attention to those modern theologians who are admittedly expert in the interpretation of the Fathers. P. Galtier states that the Fathers conceive the special presence of the inhabitation, not as a presence that results from our acts, but as an ontological presence that comes with the state of grace. "They describe this presence under the image of an application, to the substance of the just soul, of the very substance of the divine Persons and by no means as an intellectual apprehension by man of their action upon him."[36] In describing the general features of this presence, Galtier says that they can be reduced to the characteristics of an unguent which communicates itself to the soul, to a seal which imprints its image on the soul, to a principle of action which is superadded to our natural powers. The advent of God, according to the Fathers, manifests itself by a transformation of our nature. His presence not only elevates and enlarges our powers to act, but from the mere fact of his presence the very substance of our soul is deified.[37]

The common thought of the Fathers, according to Galtier, is that the Holy Spirit plays a role in the just soul similar to that played by the soul in relation to the body. That we may understand what the advent of the Spirit means the Fathers represent the Spirit as applying himself to our substance, communicating to it new energies, and completing thus its supernatural structure. "Without in any way denying that created grace is the only and the sufficient intrinsic, inherent formal cause of our justification, we must recognize also that the divine persons themselves render us holy and do so by a mysterious adhesion to our soul."[38]

The Fathers, Galtier assures us, have in view a union which is by no means a substantial union or a hypostatic union. The union of body and soul to form one complete substance is an example of a substantial union. The union of the divine and human natures in the one Person of Jesus Christ is a hypostatic union. The Holy Spirit does not inform the soul as a substantial form. When certain authors speak of the Holy Spirit as a partial formal cause of justification, however, it is evident that what they are trying to express by that vague term is the manifest doctrine of the Fathers of the Church. The Fathers taught a communication of the Divinity to the soul which is as direct and immediate as possible.[39] They unwearyingly exclude the interposition of any creature whatsoever. "The divine Persons sanctify us immediately by the immediate application of their substance to our souls. The Fathers even employ the word "form" to describe the role played by God in sanctifying man. They are obviously aware that the image engraved upon our soul by the divine "Seal" is different from the Seal Itself. The image imprinted upon wax by a seal is not the seal itself. The created image of God in our soul is not God who produces the image there. But it is the application of the Holy Spirit which produces and conserves this image, according to patristic tradition."[40]

P. Gaechter has established the fact that St. Irenaeus did not depart from this traditional doctrine of the sealing and the anointing. His expressions of our union with the Holy Spirit are in fact quite as strong as those used of the Hypostatic Union. The Holy Spirit is the object of a participation and a communion. The Spirit is united to the body and soul of man. St. Irenaeus spoke of a mixture and union of the Spirit and man, of an insertion of the Spirit into man, of an inpouring of the Spirit. P. Gaechter asks what can be the meaning of these expressions, so incomparably stronger than the more frequent "inhabit" in their suggestion of union. He replies that if one examines all the texts in which there is mention of the Spirit, one will frequently find that the gifts of the Spirit are the consequences of His union with man. Furthermore the expressions used unanimously suggest a direct union with the soul.[41]

D'Ales had already made it clear that in the mind of St. Irenaeus the Holy Spirit was inseparable from his gifts. He had also described the Holy Spirit, in St. Irenaeus's doctrine, as a "supersubstantial form which fulfills, in the supernatural order, a role similar to that which the soul fulfills in the natural order."[42]

De Regnon, describing the doctrine of St. Athanasius, implies that St. Athanasius maintained an immediate impression of the substance of the Divinity to the soul in the production of grace. "It is the substantial and personal presence of the Holy Spirit which sanctifies us, by forming in us his imprint. Obviously habitual grace is not the Holy Spirit any more than the imprint is the seal which imprints. But the presence of the seal is necessary to form the imprint and to preserve it. For the soul is like some liquid stuff that keeps the figure marked in it only so long as the seal remains in it as a sort of informing power."[43]

In concluding this brief survey of the teaching of the Fathers and of the theologians who favored the Greek theory, what can we say of evidence for formal causality in their teaching? It is clear that we cannot expect that the Fathers will use terms in the carefully restricted and defined way of scholastic theology. Nevertheless, in reading the Greek Fathers one cannot help but be impressed by several points that could be said to favor some type of formal causality. Whether it be exemplary-formal, objective-formal, or some type of intrinsic-formal causality on the part of God remains to be discussed.

The first point is the Fathers' unfailing insistence that no creature can deify man, that only the Holy Spirit or the Eternal Word, substantially present, can do so. This certainly suggests that more than the efficient causality which would be present in any case where God created or caused a created gift. It appears also that the Fathers maintain that the created gift arises precisely from the communication of the substance of the Divinity to the soul. The Holy Spirit is impressed on the soul after the fashion of a seal, and does not, so to speak act at a distance. His activity is immediate. The new created image of God is due to some immediate communication of the Spirit. A causality that is unique seems to be suggested by the patristic metaphors. It certainly appears to be in some sense formal causality that is hinted at, but whether that causality is extrinsic or in some fashion intrinsic, the Fathers do not determine, although their images, if taken literally, would suggest intrinsic causal influence of the Holy Spirit as some type of form or formal cause.

NOTES

1 K. Rahner, "Zur Begrifflichkeit der ungeschaffenen Gnade," in Z.K. Th., 1939, p. 139.
2 Ibid., p. 139.
3 P. Dumont, "Le caractère divin de la grâce," Revue des sciences religieuses, 1924, p. 92.
4 See A. d'Alès, "La doctrine de l'Esprit en Saint Irénée," Rech. de Science Religieuse, 1924, p. 528; P. Gächter, "Unsere Einheit mit Christus nach dem hl. Irenäus," Z.K. Th., 1934, pp. 503-532; Martinez-Gomez, "Relación entre la inhabitación del Espiritu santo y los donos creados de la justificación," Estudios Ecclesiasticos, 1935, pp. 20-50.
5 Thes. 34, P.G. 75, 597 c.
6 De Trin. dial. 7; P.G. 75, c. 1121.
7 De Trin., dial. 7, P.G. 75, c. 1089.
8 In Is. IV., 2; P.G. 70, 936.
9 In Joan. XI, II; P.G. 74, 554.
10 De Recta Fide; P.G. 76, 1188.
11 Athan., Ep. ad Serapionem, I, 24; P.G. 26, 585.
12 Athan., Ep. de Synodis, 51, P.G. 26, 784.
13 St. Basil, Ep. 8, 10; P.G. 32, 261.
14 St. Cyril, In Joan. I, 9; P.G. 73, 157.
15 St. Cyril, In Joan. IX, 14-17; P.G. 74, 260.

[16] *Ep. ad Serapionem*, n. 23; *P.G.* 26, 586.
[17] *Ibid.*
[18] *In Joan.* XI, 10; *P.G.* 74, 542.
[19] *In Joan.* XI, 10; *P.G.* 74, 543.
[20] *Ibid.*
[21] *In Joan.* XI, 11; *P.G.* 74, 554.
[22] *P.G.* 75, 610.
[23] *Thes.* assertio 34; *P.G.* 75, 598.
[24] *De Trin.*, dial. 7; *P.G.* 75, 1114.
[25] *Ibid.*, 1094.
[26] *Ibid.*, 1122.
[27] *Ibid.*, 1087.
[28] *Ibid.*, 1087.
[29] *Ibid.*
[30] *Ibid.*, 1089.
[31] *Adv. Eunomium*, III, 2; *P.G.* 29, 659.
[32] *De Spiritu Sancto*, XXVI, 61; *P.G.* 32, 179-180.
[33] Rahner, "Zur Begrifflichkeit der ungeschaffenen Gnade," in *Z.K. Th.*, 1939, pp. 152-153.
[34] L. Lessius, *De Summo Bono*, II, I, 4, Antwerp, Moretos, 1616.
[35] L. Lessius, *De Perfectionibus Divinis*, XII, XI, 74.
[36] Galtier, *L'Habitation en nous des trois personnes*, Roma, P.U.G., 1950, p. 202.
[37] *Ibid.*, p. 203.
[38] *Ibid.*, pp. 203-204.
[39] *Ibid.*, pp. 207-209.
[40] *Ibid.*, pp. 209-210.
[41] P. Gächter, "Unsere Einheit mit Christus nach dem hl. Irenäus," *Z.K. Th.*, LIII (1934), pp. 530-531.
[42] D'Alès, "La doctrine de l'Esprit en S. Irénée," *R. Sc. Rel.*, 1924, p. 510.
[43] De Regnon, *La Sainte Trinité*, Paris, Retaux, Etude XXVI, p. 484.

Chapter 4.   The Union of Friendship

WE have examined the data of revelation concerning the divine inhabitation and have established the position of the problem involved. We shall now proceed to a brief exposition and evaluation of the various theories offered as an explanation of this admittedly thorny problem. The writers on the divine indwelling are legion. We shall not examine each in detail. Rather we shall examine three major trends as embodied in the more modern authorities representative of these trends. The more modern authorities have generally given more systematic and more metaphysical a treatment of this question than have the older authorities.[1]

Each of the different theories, even those we may disagree with, has made a contribution toward a complete solution of the problem of the mode of the divine indwelling. Any criticism we may be inclined to make should be accompanied by a realization and an appreciation of this fact.

The outstanding theologians who have dealt with the problem of the mode of the divine indwelling may be divided into three general groups. The first group includes those who appeal to efficient causality to explain the divine inhabitation. The second group appeal to what is known as an "objective union," and the third group appeal in some way to formal causality.

The efficient-causality theory of Vasquez, a famous Spanish theologian of the sixteenth century, is today judged insufficient with practical unanimity. This theory would explain the new presence of God in the souls of the just by efficient causality alone. It is founded on the principle that God is omnipresent to creatures as their creative cause. Since he is present wherever he operates, God will be most intimately present to all creatures. The higher the created effect that God produces, the more intimately present is God to that creature. As St. John Damascene says, God is indeed everywhere but by that one means that he is present by his operation. "Whence it follows that the more a creature shares in God's operation, and his grace, the more that creature is the dwelling-place of God. Hence heaven is his home, for in heaven the angels do his will."[2] The Doctors of the Church so explain what is called God's presence of immensity. In the opinion of some, this is also how they explain his new presence in the just soul. "God is present to the just soul as the efficient and exemplary cause of its supernatural being. He remains in the just soul because his effect there is permanent and when God produces effects, he himself is present, necessarily."[3] This is practically identical with the opinion of Vasquez, according to whom God may be said to be especially present in the souls of the just since he produces there effects that he produces nowhere else. By their very nature these effects would demand his presence there even if he were present nowhere else.

To the majority of theologians this explanation has appeared insufficient. It is difficult to see, in this explanation, any essential difference between the mode of God's presence in the soul of the just man and his presence everywhere else. In both cases it is the presence of immensity, of a higher degree in the case of the just man, but specifically the same presence. The production of grace as a particular case of the production of being in general entails a presence of immensity, but nothing specifically new. A difference of degree does not seem sufficient to explain revelation's insistence on a new, substantial presence.[4]

Vasquez' contemporary, the famous Jesuit theologian and metaphysician, Suarez, had proposed a theory of the divine inhabitation which sought to explain the new presence by an appeal to the nature of perfect charity and perfect friendship. To Suarez, the soul in the state of grace has, as if by a connatural right, the intimate real and personal presence of God. Aware of the deficiency of Vasquez' theory to establish a specifically new presence, Suarez leans heavily upon the newness of God's presence to the justified soul. By virtue of grace and charity, as by a special title, the soul has God really present. Because of charity, there is established between God and the soul a most perfect friendship. Friendship, however, seeks the union of friends, not merely an intentional or ideal union, but, insofar as possible, an inseparable presence. Hence the friendship which exists between the soul and God demands the intimate presence of God to the soul. Were God not present by any other title, the friendship would suffice to make him present.

The fundamental defect of this position was early pointed out by Vasquez, who remarked that love and friendship could also exist among persons not substantially present to each other. Suarez felt, however, that by appealing to the special character of the love established between God and us by grace, he could obtain a presence that was at once new and substantial. Friendship seeks as far as possible the substantial presence of the friends involved. When one of the friends is God, there should be no obstacle in the way of his making himself really, physically, substantially present.

This appeal to the omnipotence of God, however, does not appear to advance the case. Certainly God can give himself to his creature whom he has stirred to love him and to desire his presence. The question remains: precisely how does God realize the gift of his substantial presence on this earth? Charity evidently does not answer all the questions involved. Of itself, charity seeks union but it has not been demonstrated that it can constitute God present.

Suarez' opinion has found favor, nevertheless, with a considerable number of theologians. In modern times, the French theologian, Barthelemy Froget, has revived a similar opinion and given it a more complete treatment. He makes use of two basic principles in his description of the way in which charity is the source of our union with God. The first is the nature of love itself; the second is the continuity of grace and glory. According to the teaching of the Church, grace is the beginning of glory. Since then beatitude consists in the act by which the soul takes possession of the sovereign good, and enjoys that good, it cannot fail to happen that the just man, even in this life, possessing grace, begins by his acts to enjoy God. This takes place by the quasi-experimental knowledge which is the fruit of the gift of wisdom, and especially by charity.[5]

According to this theory, it is by knowledge and love that the just soul enters into contact with the divine Substance and begins to enjoy God. For the moment we shall concern ourselves only with the presence of charity and not with the presence of knowledge. According to Froget, the charity of this earth is not specifically different from that of heaven and consequently permits an enjoyment and possession of God. "It is the very word of God which assures us that the Holy Spirit is sent to us with grace and that he dwells within us with the firm intention of remaining there. We may therefore begin at once to enjoy the fruits of his presence and his friendship."[6] Enjoyment of a person supposes that person's real presence. God is therefore really, physically, substantially present to the Christian who has grace, and it is not a simple material presence, it is a true possession accompanied by the beginning of fruition. It is a union incomparably superior to the union which binds other creatures to their Creator. It is a union surpassed only by the union of the two natures in Christ, a union which, when it has arrived at a certain stage is truly a foretaste of heavenly glory, a sort of prelude to beatitude.

Thus Froget would maintain that this explanation assured both a specifically new presence and a substantial presence, based on the continuity of grace and glory. Charity will not pass away. In heaven its flame will be enhanced by the immediate presence of the supreme good, its ardors will redouble in intensity, but its nature will not change. It is evident that in heaven charity demands a substantial presence, a real union, a consummate union of the created will with the divine good. Does it not seem natural that it also demands, on earth, the true and substantial presence of that good, that we may begin here on earth to enjoy that good, especially since charity was given us here precisely that we might enjoy that good? Froget asserts that this conclusion imposes itself on whoever reflects that charity on earth differs only in degree from charity in heaven. Although unable to know God immediately on this earth, we are able to love him as he is in himself, directly and immediately.

There are, however, serious difficulties in the way of accepting this solution. The most radical, perhaps, is the one which faced Suarez: the illegitimate transition from "demand" to "constitute". It may be very true that charity here below seeks the substantial presence of the Beloved. That is no proof, however, that charity is capable of constituting

God substantially present. Nor does the appeal to the continuity of grace and glory solve the difficulty.

Charity is indeed specifically the same in heaven and on earth. But from the specifying object of charity, God himself, we can conclude nothing about its real presence. A tendency need not be in actual possession of its term to be specified by that term. All that holds true for the state of a tendency in possession of its object is by no means automatically proven true of that tendency in every state. What is true of the state of glory is not true of the state of grace merely from the identity of the tendency involved, namely, charity.

Froget argues also from the capacity of the loving will to unite itself directly to God in fruition of God. This seems to mistake the fundamental nature of union and fruition. Fruition is rather the result of union with the satisfying object of a tendency than the cause of such a union. Fruition takes place precisely because the tendency is united to the object of its desire and can consequently enjoy that object. A thing does not become really present when the will delights in it, because the will delights in it, but rather presence is an indispensable condition necessarily presupposed to that delight. Neither in heaven nor on earth does fruition render present the beloved object. If on earth we enjoy the fruition of God in some degree, it is because he is already present prior to that fruition. The problem is to explain the how of that presence. To appeal to the fact of fruition does not advance our understanding of the modality of the presence under discussion. Love, even when perfect, seeks the presence of the beloved, seeks a real union with the beloved, but of itself, love, even fruitive love, is incapable of establishing such a union.

From the imperfect fruition which man enjoys in this life we would rather be inclined to deduce an imperfect, an intentional or merely psychological union, than a substantial presence.

Froget renews the argument of Suarez based on perfect friendship. In human love one must often be content with a mere moral or psychological union. Separation may be necessary and inevitable. But to God nothing is impossible. "Since God's all-powerful will can realize what it chooses to, we can legitimately conclude that his love for the just soul inspires in him a quasi-need to be permanently present to it."[7]

The preceding argumentation may be valid to establish the fact of the divine inhabitation, granted that the necessity leaves God free, but it tells us nothing of the way in which this inhabitation is accomplished. God who by his free gift of grace has initiated this friendship, does indeed will to fulfill the creature's longing for a real and substantial presence. He who stirred up this longing for union will satiate it completely in the joys of heaven. Here on earth he responds to the creature's longing with a substantial inhabitation. Of this divine inhabitation, however, the exigencies of love do not explain the mode. It is not sufficient to point out that charity remains specifically the same in heaven and on earth. This line of argumentation fails to take account of differences as significant as the similarities in question. The conditions of heaven and earth are different even where it is a question of charity.

In heaven man possesses the light of glory. On earth he does not. This involves a difference for charity also. In heaven the intellect can lay hold of the sovereign good and deliver it over to the delectation of charity. For even in the state of beatitude it is not charity which lays hold of the good. The role of charity is to tend to the good and when that good is present, to enjoy it, to exercise fruition. The faculty which renders an intelligible good present is the intellect and not the will. Charity is the principle of effective union, in the sense that it stirs up in the loving subject the ardent desires that move the subject to lay hold of the object by the faculties proper to effect such a possession and union. In the case of intelligible ends or objects that faculty is the intelligence and not the will.

Neither the exigencies of perfect charity nor the specific identity of earthly and heavenly charity completely satisfy the mind seeking an explanation for a presence which is at once new and substantial. Friendship tends to establish such a union but of itself it seems capable of creating only a moral, "intentional" union. The union of charity is a union of affections, and affection does not render the beloved substantially present. It is true that the power to suppress the distance between the two substantial beings involved belongs to One of the parties of the friendship in this case, but this does not solve the difficulty. Nor is the point to be established that God has suppressed the distances and achieved a substantial indwelling. The precise point to be proven is that God has achieved this indwelling through charity. This Froget's theory does not seem to have done with unqualified success.

In his explanation of the divine indwelling, Froget completes the solution of Suarez by integrating with it the principle of the specific identity of earthly and heavenly charity, but he also makes use of another solution which is not Suarezian. It was first sketched out by John of St. Thomas, one of the greatest commentators on the works of St. Thomas Aquinas. John of St. Thomas maintains that charity alone is not sufficient to explain the divine indwelling. He offers a solution which accepts the presence of immensity as a condition of the substantial presence, and then explains the newness by an appeal to man's acts of knowledge and love. This theory has come to be known as the "objective" theory, or the theory of "objective union." After John of St. Thomas it received little acceptance until recent years when it was revived by P. Gardeil and presented as the solution of St. Thomas Aquinas. Today most thomists accept this theory in one or another variation. It is our intention to discuss this theory in the next chapter, where we shall examine the views of its more able defenders.

NOTES

[1] Cf. Trutsch, S. Trinitatis inhabitatio apud theologos recentiores, Trento, 1949.
[2] St. John Damascene, De Fide Orthodoxa, L. I, c. 13; P.G., T. 94, col. 851.
[3] J. P. Terrien, "La Grace et la Gloire," Paris, Lethielleux, 1901, t. I, p. 251.
[4] Recently L. D. Sullivan has tried to establish that Vasquez has been misunderstood. See his Justification and the Inhabitation of the Holy Trinity, the Doctrine of Father Gabriel Vasquez, Rome, 1940. P.U.G.
[5] Barthelemy Froget, De l'Inhabitation du S. Esprit dans les âmes justes, Paris, Lethielleux, 1900, pp. 156-157.
[6] Ibid., pp. 156-158.
[7] Froget, op. cit., p. 171.

Chapter 5.   Objective Union

TO John of St. Thomas the impossibility of demanding of acts of knowledge and love that they render God substantially present is perfectly evident. From the fact that God is known and loved by man we cannot infer more than an intentional presence. God would have to be said to be present in man's mind. If God were not really present to us substantially, he says, we could still unite ourselves to him by acts of love and knowledge. For example, we can unite ourselves with the Blessèd Virgin and with the saints who are not substantially present to us. Nor do our acts of faith and love here render them physically, substantially present to us. It remains for us to seek elsewhere the basis of the new substantial presence that is had in the divine indwelling.[1]

John of St. Thomas will nevertheless follow the traditional formula that God is present, "as one known in the mind of the knower, as one loved in the will of the lover." Essentially his point of view is a synthesis of the solutions of Vasquez and Suarez. These authors had presented two factors to explain the divine inhabitation. The contribution of Vasquez was the presence of immensity, resulting from the fact that God operates to produce and conserve grace. The contribution of Suarez was the intrinsic exigency of charity and grace demanding a new presence, but seemingly unable to constitute such a new presence or to account for its substantial character. The approach of John of St. Thomas is to combine these two elements in a synthesis.

In this theory our acts of knowledge and love are not required to fill the function of bringing God really present—for the simple reason that he is already present by his immensity. He himself is present in the soul of the just man, substantially present as creator and conserver of man's being. But our acts of knowledge and love have a very important function. It is in the exercise of these acts that we attain to possess, in a new way, the Divinity already present within us by immensity. The possibility of God becoming newly present to us as the object of knowledge and love lies precisely in His presence to us by immensity. This presence of immensity, based on efficient causality, is itself the basis for another presence as its necessary presupposition. For the new presence results from a direct and immediate perception of the God already substantially present by his immensity. The first presence thus explains the substantial character of the divine indwelling and the immediate perception of the first presence accounts for what is special in the new presence.

According to John of St. Thomas the dynamism of charity and grace plus the substantial character of the presence by immensity must be synthesized to offer any complete account of a divine indwelling which is both new presence and substantial presence. The point of departure is the presence of immensity but it is faith, charity and above all the gift of wisdom which permit the just soul to enjoy the experiential knowledge of the God so present.

This experiential knowledge of God is considered indirect or "quasi-experiential" by certain modern exponents of the theory of objective union. Here they are more in accord with St. Thomas himself than with John of St. Thomas. Others consider the knowledge to be in some way direct, as did John of St. Thomas himself.

Froget compares the experiential knowledge in question with the quasi-experiential knowledge the human soul has of itself. In the present state of union with the body, he says, the soul does not know itself directly and by intuition. It does not see its own essence. But it infers its own existence from its acts, since it is the principle of those acts. There is however a difference between the soul's knowledge of its own existence and its knowledge of any other soul's existence. To the knowledge of another soul's existence we proceed by means of deduction from external acts which manifest a vital principle. To know our own soul we also appeal to deduction but in this case we argue from facts of an internal order. We do not merely conclude to its existence. We feel life within us. We are conscious of our thoughts, of our decisions, of all those movements of which we are at once the witnesses and the principles.[2] The knowledge of our soul as principle of our acts may be called quasi-experiential, because it remains "indirect, obscure and deductive."[3]

In a proportionate manner, in Froget's view, we may be said to have quasi-experiential knowledge of God dwelling in the soul by virtue of the gift of wisdom. Faith alone would not suffice. What we need is a knowledge that results from a gift appropriated to the Holy Spirit, a knowledge that renders us like to the Person of the Holy Spirit, a knowledge in some way experiential, which is acquired only by intimate union with God in charity, a knowledge which is the first fruit of the gift of wisdom.[4]

The weakest point in Froget's explanation of the new presence seems to be just this indirect quality of the knowledge involved. Froget rightly insists that the knowledge is indirect. But such a knowledge would seem to be an insufficient basis on which to found a new substantial presence. In order that God himself, in his divine reality, become substantially present to us we would need more than an indirect knowledge, remaining within the framework of Froget's theory. In the Beatific Vision we have a new presence based on the direct and unmediated application of God to the soul. But where the knowledge remains indirect, it would seem that we are in contact with a created likeness or a concept of God, not with God himself. The knowledge would appear, at least, to be intentional. God would be present in a mental way as the object of our act of knowledge. An intentional or mental presence is not sufficient to explain the new presence of the divine inhabitation, and it is hardly satisfactory simply to assert without proof that in the present instance the presence is more than intentional.

Unless the quasi-experiential knowledge here in question possesses the immediacy that theologians reserve to the Beatific Vision, and admittedly it cannot, then Froget's explanation lacks the supra-intentional or supra-conceptual presence it must explain. The physical reality of God applied in a direct, unmediated contact to the human intelligence would bring God present to a man in a substantial way. As Froget's theory now stands, however, it has not demonstrated that without such an application we have any more than an intentional union and presence. Even a man without faith and a sinner with faith may have an intentional presence. The new presence of God within the soul of the just man therefore cannot be explained in a way that implies no more than an intentional presence.

Perhaps the most complete, and one of the most profound expositions of the objective theory of John of St. Thomas has been developed by P. Gardeil.[5] According to Gardeil, the presence of immensity is always presupposed to any other mode of divine presence, including the presence of grace. Insofar as grace is a created reality, it falls under the law of all created being. It demands the presence of God by power, presence and immensity to explain its existence and conservation. It is precisely this presence of immensity which is to lend a substantial character to the divine inhabitation. The physical reality of God will be present by immensity. Grace, insofar as it is being, insofar as it is opposed to nothing, requires the exercise of God's efficient causality to produce and to conserve it. This involves a presence which theologians call the presence of immensity.

Grace as a supernatural entity, however, is also to be explained by efficient causality, if we are considering its production and conservation. We are advised by Gardeil not to make the mistake of thinking that this presence of immensity brings the Triune God formally present as Triune. By the presence of immensity it is the One God who is present as efficient cause. "The production of grace does not change the nature of God's presence by efficient causality or operation, but it does extend and accentuate this presence."[6] By the very fact that God produces in us his divine grace and the accompanying virtues, he is substantially present to the soul, and it is useless to seek elsewhere the substantial character of the divine indwelling. God is present as efficient cause, and he is present substantially in no other way. "It seems impossible to discover any other way in which God could unite himself to the human soul."[7]

In one phrase Gardeil clarifies the role played by the presence of immensity: the role of grace is to ordain us to rejoin God in a new way ... the God already present to us by immensity.

That grace, as being, demands the exercise of efficient causality and hence involves God's presence of immensity, a substantial presence, may be readily admitted. But what of the other two suppositions? Is grace as a supernatural entity purely the result of efficient causality? And is it true that substantial presence is conceivable only on the basis of efficient causality, only as presence of immensity? We shall deal with these questions later.

If for the sake of discussion for the time being we grant these two presuppositions of P. Gardeil, we can then study his attempt to demonstrate how the just soul has an immediate and direct perception of the God who dwells substantially within it. He will explain the newness of the presence in the divine indwelling by an experiential knowledge and love. Unlike Froget, however, Gardeil will maintain that this experiential knowledge is somehow direct and immediate. The experiential knowledge makes the presence new; the presence of immensity insures that this specifically new presence is a substantial presence or inhabitation. Faith, charity and above all the gift of wisdom permit to the soul an experiential perception of the God within, so that a true fruition results.

Gardeil distinguishes three stages of this knowledge and love of God. The lowest stage is that possessed by baptized infants. This is the stage at which God is possessed as an "habitual object." God is unconsciously present, although the infant exercises no activity of knowledge and love.

The second stage is that where the soul exercises its activity under the domination of faith, charity and the gift of wisdom, and achieves a knowledge, which while intimate, can still be called intentional or mediate.

The third stage brings us to the fullness of what Gardeil calls experimental (experiential) knowledge. In this stage the soul reflects upon itself as principle, with God, of its acts of faith and love. Here, the soul attains to a direct, supra-intentional, immediate knowledge of the Divinity substantially dwelling within.

The divine indwelling thus obtained presupposes the substantial presence of God in the soul. By acts of knowledge and love God is seized anew in his substantial reality.

While the theory of P. Gardeil has attracted many admirers, it has also met with criticisms, and even from within the thomist school.[8] To many the objective theory seems to achieve a presence which is at best intentional, psychological, moral.

Many authors have criticized Gardeil's theory by attaching their criticism almost exclusively to the question of the "habitual object." Perhaps an even more fundamental difficulty, however, lies in the nature of the immediate knowledge of God that this theory claims for the just soul. A third difficulty arises even if an immediate knowledge of God is admitted. It is difficult to see how such an experiential knowledge would make possible a substantial presence which would be new precisely as substantial. We shall now discuss briefly each of these three difficulties.

The first difficulty concerns the habitual object. The contention of the adversaries of any theory which relies exclusively on an objective union is that such a theory leaves infants in grace devoid of a new substantial presence. This is a serious charge. If it is true then such a theory cannot be accepted.

If the new substantial presence of God is attributed to acts of knowledge and love, what becomes of this new presence in the case of infants? The usual reply is that the infant, possessing the infused virtues, possesses God newly present as an habitual object. The infant does not have an actual consciousness of God substantially present. God is substantially present, however, and the infant possesses the "habit" or permanent disposition which will enable it at a later date to become conscious of the presence of which it is now unconscious. In a somewhat similar fashion a mathematician is said to possess the object of mathematics as an habitual object, and himself to have the habit of mathematics, even though he may not be actually engaged in conscious mathematical activity at a given time.

The difficulty is a real one for the divine indwelling of which revelation speaks is not one reserved to the few who in this life are gifted with mystical graces that would make possible the direct contact of which Gardeil speaks. In no case can the infant make these acts that create the new presence. Yet the infant cannot be excluded from the gift of the divine inhabitation. In Gardeil's personal exposition of the objective theory the difficulty appears to be aggravated. For in Gardeil's theory the direct, immediate knowledge, whose function is to make God newly present, seems to be reserved to the mystical states, which relatively few just men seem to attain.

In its actual state the just soul cannot ordinarily become aware of the God who offers Himself to it as an object of knowledge and love. Not to speak of the infant for the moment, the ordinary just soul whose spiritual life is not a mystic's, is gifted only with a power to know God directly. We must note that this power, this potency, normally only passes into act, becomes actual, after many years of fervent preparation.

Previous to the direct perception of God the just soul does know an effective union with God but this union remains in the intentional or mental order. It is a union by similitudes or concepts. Consequently it is unable to effect the substantial indwelling revelation requires. Only the direct, immediate contact, not a contact through concepts, renders God so substantially present, on Gardeil's own admission. Even "ordinary" mystical contemplation has its source in the conceptual activity of formed faith, and is therefore incapable of a direct perception of God, which perception alone, according to Gardeil, can render God newly present in the way required.

This brings us precisely to the difficulty of the habitual object. The divine indwelling comes with grace. It is not something which rare souls may gain upon rare occasions. Revelation speaks of an inhabitation which is had by the very fact that grace is had. However weak the spiritual life of a soul may be, however far removed from a mystical experience of God, if that soul possesses sanctifying grace, it possesses the Trinity indwelling. This is the inhabitation we are concerned with: the inhabitation proper to all just souls insofar as they are just and not a mystical possession of God which is the joy and treasure of the few. The newly baptized infant who has made no act of love or knowledge is truly the living temple of the Holy Spirit and no theory which endangers this truth can be accepted. It will easily enough be admitted that the infant does not enjoy a direct, immediate experience of the presence of God. If it is this knowledge alone that effects the divine indwelling, it seems that the Holy Trinity is absent from the soul of the baptized infant.

Moreover the ordinary man in the state of grace, even if he is advanced to ordinary mystical prayer, does not, in Gardeil's opinion, have the direct and immediate experience of God, "which alone assures their (the Divine Persons) presence."[9] Hence it would appear that God is newly present only in those souls who have passed beyond ordinary mystical prayer.

The defenders of an objective union maintain that the ordinary Christian, who does not possess any actual experiential knowledge, nonetheless does possess such knowledge "habitually." In Gardeil, this habitual knowledge is quite clearly a potency and nothing more. In the actual state of affairs the disproportion between the intellectual energy of the soul and the divine object it is destined to embrace renders the soul incapable of more than an intentional, a conceptual union with God indwelling. It is true that this habitual knowledge is not without its connatural inclination to realize its potentialities, but for the infant and the man who has not yet passed beyond the ordinary mystical prayer, this realization does not take place. In its present state the soul cannot know God directly as present. It is merely "capable" of this knowledge which is to render God newly present. Capable here seems to reduce itself to a remote potentiality. The actuation of this potency depends upon many conditions that are not verifiable in all souls having grace. "... The experiential knowledge which should assure the substantial presence of God, is purely 'habitual' for most souls. Adults seem no better favored than infants."[10]

The habitual knowledge exists from the moment the faculty of intellect is present to an object of knowledge which it is capable of perceiving at some future time. When it will please God to manifest himself, just souls will know and love him immediately. Before that these souls are "capable" of such immediate knowledge. But since Gardeil himself ascribes the divine indwelling to actual and not potential knowledge, it looks as though most justified souls will be forever deprived on earth of the divine indwelling.

Garrigou-Lagrange unwittingly exposed the weakness of this notion of the habitual object when he wrote: "In order that this presence be actually had, it suffices that God be in the just soul ... as an object which can be known by quasi-experiential knowledge, that is, as an object not distant. It is not necessary that he be known in an actual way."[11] What can be the significance of the phrase, "that God be present in the just soul?" The precise problem is not whether it suffices for God to be present or not—but whether he is present if we accept an objective theory. The only "presence" we can speak of as already accomplished, in Garrigou-Lagrange's view, is the presence of immensity. Every Catholic theologian grants that presence. To then argue that God is present in a new substantial way, that this presence is "realized" because God is "knowable" experientially seems at least misleading. A mere power to know God quasi-experientially does not render God present to the child who cannot actualize this power now. What can be the meaning of the phrase, "as an object not distant?" God is indeed not distant; by his immensity he is present. What we are trying to explain is a new presence. No presence beyond that of immensity has yet been established by the theory of an objective union.

Recognizing the importance of this difficulty of the habitual object, most defenders of an objective theory spend considerable time explaining it away. Various ingenious attempts, notably those of R. Morency[12] and S.I. Dockx, O.P.,[13] have been made to render the idea of an habitual object plausible, but no explanation seems satisfactory. The same difficulty plagues every defender of an objective theory. Granted that God is not present, except by the presence of immensity, in the unbaptized child, we must explain how he becomes present at baptism, newly, substantially present. Somehow all objective theorists appeal to acts; in the absence of acts they appeal to a power some day to produce these acts, to an ultimate disposition to produce these acts. The problem is then only pushed back one step. How does a capacity to produce acts in the future render God present now? How does a "habit", an ultimate disposition to produce acts of knowledge or love render God objectively present now? This difficulty it seems remains to perturb all systems of objective divine inhabitation.

A second problem connected with the theory of an objective inhabitation is the problem of immediacy. The difficulty of an immediate knowledge of God is particularly conspicuous in the theory of P. Gardeil. He seems to recognize that an indirect and mediate knowledge cannot constitute God newly present in his substantial reality. That the divine substance become present in itself and not through the intermediaries of concepts it must enter into immediate contact with the soul. Otherwise a created similitude is present, God is present "intentionally", or morally, but not in his own reality. Such an "intentional" presence is usually ascribed to faith, formed and unformed, and therefore cannot be the presence of grace.

It seems then necessary in Gardeil's theory that the physical reality of God be somehow immediately applied to the created intellect. If the substance of the Divinity is to play the role of an objective termination of the human intellect, that substance must, in its substantial reality be directly applied to the intellect.

Clearly a mental image does not give us the presence of the thing it represents except as the signified in the sign. This presence, being of the intentional order, leaves the object, in its physical reality, at a distance. The image may be more or less perfect than the philosopher's, but both, remaining mediate, leave their object in its physical reality at a distance. The just man's knowledge of faith is more perfect than the sinner's, but both are mediate knowledge, and as mediate knowledge they leave their object at a distance. As long as knowledge takes place by means of similitudes it will not render God present in his substantial reality.

The contact with God by similitudes, the intentional contact, is insufficient to deify us, to explain a substantial indwelling. A sinner may make an act of faith. He does not thereby obtain divine grace. He does not thereby obtain the divine inhabitation proper to the state of grace. To convey the Divinity to the soul there must be contact of being, immediate knowledge or some other form of immediate contact of the Divinity and the soul.

At first glance it seems almost obvious that an immediate knowledge of God in this life is impossible. If the divine essence were present in knowledge in this life, it is difficult to see why we would not have the Beatific Vision. It is true that the advocates of such an immediate knowledge usually maintain that the knowledge is "obscure", but obscurity seems to touch only the degree of the vision and not its essence. If the vision is had, clear or obscure, one has passed beyond the type of knowledge theologians usually admit for man in this life—unless a man be favored with the rarest of mystical graces—and we are not discussing such exceptional cases but the inhabitation common to all the just. In our earthly knowledge of God, save for extraordinary cases, it would seem that an objective intermediary must intervene. It is difficult to see how an immediate knowledge, such as Gardeil defends, can be admitted as the basis of a theory of the divine indwelling. It is exceedingly rare that such a knowledge is given and we must explain an inhabitation common to all the just not excluding the most unmystical. This difficulty is not shared by all exponents of an objective theory, at least not in the same open way. It is however a difficulty that is explicitly involved in the theory of John of St. Thomas whom most objective theorists claim as patron.

Besides these two difficulties of the habitual object and the immediacy of our knowledge of God, there is another weakness in the theory of John of St. Thomas and of all who follow him. John of St. Thomas and Gardeil maintain that their theory represents a synthesis, so to speak, of Suarez and Vasquez. They maintain in the line of Vasquez that the presence of immensity must enter into our explanation of the new presence of grace. They also maintain, in the line of Suarez, that it is our acts, acts of knowledge and love, that render this presence a new one. Thus for Gardeil, the presence of immensity, due to efficient causality, has the task of accounting for the substantiality of the new presence. The newness of this presence is explained by our power to know the God of immensity so substantially present in our soul by his efficient causality.

Would an immediate knowledge of the God of immensity, were such a knowledge possible to all, be sufficient, however, to explain the divine indwelling of which revelation speaks? If one does not admit the presence of immensity to give substantially to the inhabitation, then the divine inhabitation loses its substantial character. As M. Rétailleau points out,[14] the very nature of experiential knowledge is such that this knowledge does not alter the object known, but "gives" the object as it exists to the mind. If then the soul reflecting upon its supernatural acts, experiences the God of immensity present in the soul, it will not bring God newly present, it will know the God already present. A new knowledge may result from experience. But experience is not capable of rendering the reality of God newly present in a substantial way. A new substantial presence is not obtainable by experiential knowledge. A new presence, yes. A new substantial presence, new as formally substantial, no. Experience does not alter the object of experience but gives it as it exists. But in Gardeil's theory, God is present as he is present in a stone, a horse, a sinner without faith. The God of immensity is now perceived present by an experiential knowledge. Surely we can say that there results a new objective presence of the God of immensity, but a new substantial presence, a new substantial presence of the Trinity formally as triune, not simply as efficient cause? It does not seem so. The experience of the God of immensity does not constitute the Trinity newly substantially present.

It is true, as Gardeil points out in answer to this difficulty, that there are not two Gods, the God of immensity and the Triune God. But the fact that there is but one divine substance does not rule out several substantial presences of that one substance. The reality of sacramental presence testifies to this. Present substantially by immensity, God is indicated in revelation to be newly substantially present in the just soul as triune. Formally speaking God is not present in the just soul as triune because of his efficient causality there, any more than he is formally present in the stone as triune because of his efficient causality in the stone.

Moreover if God as efficient cause is perceived by the soul in its acts, why restrict this perception to the perception of God as co-principle of our supernatural acts of knowledge and love? Why, if God is perceived as efficient cause, is he also not perceived as the first cause of our muscular activity?

S. Dockx has pointed to another weakness in the theory of Gardeil.[15] Gardeil appeals to an analogy: as the soul knows itself, in its essence, immediately, so the just soul knows God, the principle, with it, of its supernatural operations. Both knowledges are experiential and immediate. As Dockx points out, however, our self-knowledge is not so much of the essence of the soul, quidditative knowledge, but knowledge of the existence of the soul. The foundation of the analogy seems to be invalid. There is also another important difference in the situation of self-knowledge and knowledge of God as principle of our supernatural acts. In knowing ourselves as the principle of our acts, we are knowing one who is at once intrinsic principle and subject of these acts. But in the divine indwelling we are dealing with a duality of subjects. We cannot experience God as subject of these acts. God is a subject distinct from us. He is not a subject which we can experience as subject. We can know him only as object, as a subject distinct from us, as a subject which presents itself to us as an object, that is, in an objective manner. Such an objective presence, however, does not result in us from God's presence as efficient cause. God is the object of knowledge as an intelligible form, as is any other object of knowledge, not as efficient cause.

It would not be correct to ascribe to every theory of the divine indwelling which explains the indwelling as an objective union all the difficulties encountered in Gardeil's explanation, although this explanation has become somewhat classic among objective theories. More recently S. Dockx has offered an interesting variation of the objective theory. His views have received deservedly wide attention. They are based primarily upon an analysis of acts of love, and only by a detour, so to speak, on acts of cognition.

It is not possible to go into detail, but it does not appear that Dockx's attempt to establish a divine indwelling through love has been completely successful. His theory has many things to commend it. It places the problem clearly. It stresses that nothing short of the un-mediated presence of the Divinity can deify us. It refuses to depend upon the identity of grace and glory so exclusively as to leave us with a potential deification that will be actual only when grace has evolved into glory. But it does not answer the classic difficulty of the habitual object and its argumentation is weak in its central point. It relies too heavily on a parallelism between knowledge and love which is not as complete as it is made out to be.

The difficulty with all theories of an objective union is that they depend upon our acts of knowledge and love, not only for a new posses-sion of the God newly present by grace, but to render God so present in a new substantial way. They have not been successful, however, in ex-plaining that new presence of the substance of the Divinity that revelation indicates as taking place with the advent of grace to the soul. One cannot explain the divine indwelling if one neglects the "objective" side, the new possession. But equally important is the aspect of the problem which is concerned with explaining the substantial presence. The theories of an exclusively objective union so emphasize the possession of God had in grace that they forget the absolute necessity of ensuring to all just souls a new substantial presence of the divine reality unique to the state of grace.

NOTES

[1] John of St. Thomas, *De Trinitate Mysterio,* q. 43, disp. 37, a. 3.

[2] Froget, *op. cit.,* pp. 182-183.

[3] *Ibid.*

[4] *Ibid.,* p. 180.

[5] See Gardeil, *La Structure de l'Âme et l'Expérience Mystique,* and the articles defending his position in the *Revue Thomiste* for March-April 1928, May-June 1929, July-September and November-December 1931.

[6] Gardeil, *Structure,* II, p. 31.

[7] *Ibid.,* p. 54, 72, 73.

[8] Among Gardeil's critics are Van der Meersch, Hugon, Vandenbroucke, Dockx, Wm. O'Connor, Urdanoz, Rétailleau, Menendez-Reigada, Rutloff.

[9] See Galtier, *De l'Habitation,* pp. 166-180.

[10] Galtier, *op. cit.,* p. 171.

[11] Garrigou-Lagrange, *Revue Thomiste,* 1928, p. 463.

[12] R. Morency, *L'Union de Grâce selon S. Thomas,* Montreal, Studio Collegii Maximi Immaculatae Conceptionis, 1950.

[13] S. I. Dockx, O.P., *Fils de Dieu par Grâce,* Paris, Desclee, 1948. Cf. also Dockx's article in N.R.T., LXXXII (1950), pp. 673-89.

[14] M. Rétailleau, *La Sainte Trinité dans les âmes justes,* Angers, Univ. Cath., 1932, p. 185.

[15] Dockx, *op. cit.,* p. 50.

Chapter 6.   The Production of Grace

TWO modern theologians, P. Galtier[1] and P. Rétailleau,[2] have both criticized the objective theory of P. Gardeil and his followers and have offered solutions of their own based on what they consider to be the unique efficient causality involved in the production of grace. The theory of Rétailleau partly depends heavily upon the solution of Galtier. We therefore shall treat Galtier's view first and then consider the additions and modifications of Rétailleau.

There is an admirable reticence in the theory of Galtier, a reticence which has misled some of his critics. There is no monumental architecture of systematic development imposed upon the data of revelation. Galtier's whole effort is to disengage what revelation has suggested about the divine indwelling and to formulate this clearly in metaphysical terms. Where he feels unable further to analyze the type of causality involved in the production of grace, he says so. "It matters little that we lack the proper term to describe the union between God and the just soul."[3]

Galtier begins his analysis of the problem by a description of the qualities tradition shows us in the presence of the divine inhabitation. This presence, he says, is of the ontological order. The Fathers conceive it as realized by the passage from sin to grace. They describe it under the form of an application to the soul of the very substance of the divine persons. It appears in tradition, not as the effect of knowledge and love, but as the cause of the new knowledge and love of which the just are capable, as the condition for the very possibility of a new objective union.

This presence has as its purpose to enable the just man to realize a more and more perfect friendship with God. From this presence of grace there flow new faculties of knowledge and love—but these faculties proceed from the new presence of the divine persons in the soul and not vice versa.

Using the very terminology of tradition, Galtier describes this presence as due to the action of God acting on the soul as an ointment acts on the body, imparting to it its own sweetness and perfume; as a seal acts, which imprints its image on another substance; as a principle of life and action superadded to our natural principle of life and action. By the very presence of the Divinity so sealing us we are deified. The Trinity —by appropriation the Holy Spirit—acts as a supersubstantial form which plays in us, in the supernatural order, a role similar to that played in the natural order by the soul. The Divinity applies itself to our soul directly, molding our soul to its image.

While emphasizing the Uncreated Gift which is conferred along with grace, we cannot, says Galtier, speak here of a substantial union. God and the soul do not fuse into a single substance. Nor can we speak of an informing, properly so-called, of the soul by the divine substance. God cannot unite himself to the soul in such wise as to qualify the soul in its being, as grace qualifies the soul. Were this to happen there would be a confusion of substances. Galtier does not consider the term "physical" union especially happy either, except insofar as it clarifies the point that the union of grace is not a mere moral union. The union of the soul and God is certainly not merely moral. The gift of the divine persons consists in a direct and immediate communication of the divine substance to the soul ... as direct a communication as is possible under the circumstances. The Fathers of the Church, Galtier explains, exclude the interposition of any creature between God and the soul. Rather it is by the application of their own substance that the divine persons sanctify us, say the Fathers, who even use the word "form". They attribute the image of the Trinity in the soul to the continued application of the Spirit to the soul, as a seal must be applied continually to liquid wax, if the wax is to retain the image of the seal.

The conclusion which Galtier derives from such statements of the Fathers may be summarized as follows: "The presence of God in the just soul is essentially an ontological presence. There can be joined to it, and usually is, a moral union or an objective presence, but this is not essential. When the Fathers of the Church proved the divinity of the Holy Spirit from our sanctification, from our sharing in the substance of his person, they implied an ontological presence. It is precisely this ontological presence that we must explain."[4]

From his analysis of the characteristics of the presence of the divine inhabitation, Galtier draws three conclusions: this presence, since it is common to all the just alike, must take place at justification and not later; this presence must be a substantial presence other than that of immensity since it is exclusively reserved for the just; it is a presence which assures an amicable possession, not a mere material presence but a true, amicable possession.

These are the data of the problem. The next step is an interpretation of the data. It is the operation of God peculiar to the production of grace which, according to Galtier, will explain the mode of the divine indwelling. This operation is of a special order, of a transcendent character which makes it singular among the works of God. For grace is not properly or exclusively the result of God's efficient causality. Although really distinct from the divine substance, grace cannot be conceived as separate from God, as existing apart from the divine substance. God is present to other things by his immensity. They require that he be so present to sustain them in existence. Their contingency demands this presence. But grace demands God's presence because of the very way that it is produced. If we could conceive God as acting where he is not present, then we could conceive of other creatures existing apart from him. Not so with grace however. Its very concept would still involve the presence of God. Why? "An image of God, grace can only be produced by the direct and immediate application of the substance of the Trinity to the soul."[5]

From this image of the seal, this impression, comes the attribution to the divine persons "... of a certain formal causality at work in our justification."[6] The presence of grace, the image, is inconceivable without the presence of the seal, the Trinity, which constantly impresses its own

likeness on the soul. "Grace implies exemplary causality more than efficient. In the case of grace the identity between efficient and exemplary
causality is formal."[7] In other cases, an exemplary cause works through
the efficient cause; here it exercises its causality by itself. In the ordinary
situation, in other words, a seal, as exemplary cause, would be impressed
on wax by someone who, as efficient cause, would operate with the seal
to apply it to the wax. In the case of grace, the Trinity is the seal impressing itself on the soul.

Galtier admits the difficulty of classifying this type of causality. "It
is not really too important that we cannot classify neatly the precise type
of causality that is at work here. Even the creation of natural effects
escapes our classification. Why should not the production of grace also
transcend our concepts?"[8]

The production of the virtue of charity considered in itself and not
in its act, brings the Holy Spirit substantially present. This, says Galtier,
is the clear teaching of St. Thomas in *Contra Gentiles*, IV, 18, and 21, 3.
St. Thomas would then recognize in the production of grace an act
properly assimilative, an act which by its very nature demands and explains the special presence of God in the just soul.

The image of God ordinarily produced by efficient causality is, says
Galtier, of such a nature that we could call it an image which, as image,
is produced, as it were, almost unintentionally. If it were possible for
the Creator to create without rendering perceptible in the creature that
wisdom and intelligence which presided over the creation, then his
image would not be discovered in ordinary creatures. But in the case
of grace this assimilation is deliberately intended. It is the purpose
and term of the divine operation. It is also a resemblance to God incomparably more perfect than is had in any other creature. The act of
producing grace, instead of, so to speak, terminating at what one might
call the surface of the Divine Being, by which he acts outside of himself,
reaches to the depths of his divine life. Hence it is that, although the
action is common to the entire Trinity, the image produced reflects the
personal characteristics of the three persons.

This operation by which God renders himself present to the creature
does not only render the creature like to God. It also renders the soul
a possessor of God in a very real sense. Grace as a principle of activity,

is ordered to action. It is an image that reflects the intellectuality of the divine nature. It is an image that makes us capable of knowing and loving God, that is, of possessing God in a new way, as God knows and loves himself. Grace is ordained to union, to the union of the Beatific Vision. The refashioning of our soul that takes place when God produces grace there is ordered to this intimate life with him. We possess that which we can use and enjoy at our discretion. By the sole fact of our justification that possession of which revelation speaks is accomplished, for we have God present and we have new faculties to enjoy him. He has come with grace, he remains as a guest with whom we may have friendly intercourse, by the acts which spring from this very grace. "This is precisely the great benefit of the state of grace. By itself alone, independently of any acts, it assures the presence of the inhabitation, and the real possession of God."[9]

One can indeed now speak of an habitual knowledge and an habitual love, once the created gift which will enable the soul to make these acts is present, with the Uncreated Gift that is inseparable from it. But, of course, by habitual knowledge one actually means the possibility to know. This does not imply that any concrete act of knowledge has actually been placed and it by no means authorizes us to say that God has been made present by such habitual knowledge. In Galtier's view, the possibility of this knowledge depends on God's new presence in the soul. Obviously then the knowledge cannot be invoked to explain that presence.

The theory of Galtier has many advantages. It tries not to go beyond what can be solidly established on the foundation of revelation and of sound metaphysical principles. It shows evidence of a profound familiarity with the Fathers, and it is marked by sobriety in the interpretation of texts. Unfortunately it also has certain serious limitations. It does not pursue very far the investigation into the metaphysics of the type of causality at stake in the production of grace. Its exploration of the relation between created and uncreated grace is very brief. While it presents us with a good organization of and evaluation of the data of revelation it does not sufficiently concern itself with a systematic effort to interpret the data at any length in terms of metaphysics, nor when such an attempt is made, can it be called particularly successful.

Galtier evidently wishes to describe the type of causality at work in the production of grace as a special type of efficient causality. This "specialness" seems to consist in two characteristics. First, we cannot separate, even conceptually, the divine presence from the production of grace. Secondly, the similitude of God expressed in the effect, grace, is in the unique case of grace, deliberately willed. Galtier thus wishes to lay peculiar stress on the exemplary causality that is at work in the production of grace, and to identify this with efficient causality.

What can be said for this option of efficient-exemplary causality? Perhaps the first thing that occurs to mind is the fact that the causality concretely described by Galtier and that described in his many citations from the Fathers is not necessarily efficient causality. In fact it looks very little like efficient causality as we know that causality. The proper note of efficient causality is to produce its effect by its action. The proper note of the causality which Galtier describes is clearly self-communication, self-donation, a sharing of the proper perfection of the cause with the effect. All of this is as clear a description as one can find of the proper note of formal causality.

Let us take one of the patristic examples. The Trinity applies itself to the soul in the production of grace as the seal is applied to the hot wax. In this process, an agent applies the seal, in the created order, but it is the seal which directly communicates its own form, an accidental form in the example. The seal obviously applies its own accidental perfection, the figure it bears, to the matter in question. The process by which the specific perfection of the seal is communicated to the matter of the wax is a combination of efficient and formal causality. Efficient causality is required to put the seal in the position where it will be possible for the seal to exert its own causality, but the direct process of transferring its form to the wax is an exercise of formal causality on the part of the seal. In no other way than by virtue of formal causality can the proper and specific perfection of the seal be so communicated to the matter in question. "An imprint engraved by the Trinity of the Trinity"—the suggestion here is clearly that the Trinity acts as a formal cause, communicating its specific perfection to the soul. The soul is divinized, say the Fathers, as iron is turned to flaming metal in a fire. The fire communicates its fieryness to the iron until the iron, while remaining iron, is scarcely to be distinguished from the fire. So it is with many patristic images: the unction of the perfume communicating its own sweetness to the anointed substance, the light that renders lightsome the space it penetrates, communicating of itself, giving of its own perfection, of its own form to the substance it transforms. There is present constantly the note of self-donation, or self-communication, of a sharing of one's own perfection with the affected substance.

Galtier himself seems to recognize this note of formal causality that rings through the Fathers. He says, "The Fathers of the Church unwearyingly exclude the mediation of any creature whatsoever in the production of grace. It is by applying their proper substance immediately to the just soul that the divine persons sanctify."[10]

He reminds us that tradition shows us the divine persons as the ray of light which penetrates the crystal, rendering the crystal brilliant with its own brilliance, conferring upon the crystal its own perfection and splendor. He tells us that Irenaeus had seen the Holy Spirit as a supersubstantial form, a form which fulfills in the supernatural order, a function similar to the function of the soul, the form, in the natural order. He assures us that this mentality is the mentality common to the Fathers, and his own interpretation of the patristic tradition throws his truth into strong relief. Petavius had said already that the Holy Spirit is shown in the Fathers to play in some way the role of a form. St. Basil says explicitly that in some mysterious way the Holy Spirit has the character of a form in his divinizing activity in our soul.

Certainly we can understand the use of the word form by the Fathers. What better word could be found to describe the direct, unmediated application of a substance to another substance with the communication of the perfection of the first substance to the second substance? As Galtier says so well, the process of our divinization is an assimilative process—we are assimilated to the perfection of the divine substance.

Yet, when he wishes to label this causality in scholastic terms, Galtier calls it efficient—exemplary causality. Certainly it should not be called material causality, nor final. Is it then by exclusion efficient—exemplary causality? Exemplary causality is an extrinsic causality, a causality that works through the mind of the agent or efficient cause. An exemplar is essentially an idea. It does not work by direct, unmediated application of itself to the matter. All the immediate self-communication which Galtier has analyzed with such painstaking care in tradition can hardly be described as the causality of an idea, an intellectual form, a cause in the ideal order. In short, if there is one idea that Galtier has successfully isolated from tradition it is the idea of self-communication, of sealing, of self-communication by self-donation of the very substance of the Trinity. To describe this as a causality in the ideal order is hardly exact. No more perfect, no more classic description of formal causality has yet been invented than these precise formulas. Why then call the causality efficient—exemplary?

Perhaps the reason may appear too obvious to need mention. God cannot be an intrinsic form of the created substance, limited and contracted to the potency of the matter he informs. The soul in man, for example, is such a form, with respect to man's body. Certainly no such intrinsic formal causality is possible to the Divinity. Yet, if the data of revelation suggest formal causality in such strong terms, would it not be preferable further to investigate explicitly the notion of formal causality, purifying it of the imperfections due to its created nature in the created order and examining whether it is then possible to apply so purified a notion to the Divinity in its exercise of divinization? This is the procedure that theologians have always followed when applying efficient causality to God as, for example, when they discuss the idea of creation. Before one could legitimately conclude in favor of efficient—exemplary causality he would have to follow such a procedure. Having then excluded this type of intrinsic formal causality, he would be in a position to undertake to demonstrate, if it is possible, that the type of causality the Fathers have described may legitimately be called some form of efficient-exemplary causality. In our opinion, this is a task that is impossible, however, for the reasons indicated in our analysis of the theory of Vasquez and in our analysis, in the present chapter, of the metaphysical structure and character of the causality in question.

A number of theologians have rallied to Galtier's point of view in more than one detail.[11] An interesting variation of Galtier's theory is the one constructed by Rétailleau. The latter insists that the crux of this difficult problem of the causality at work in the divine indwelling lies in the fact, often overlooked, that grace as being and grace as grace are due to two different causalities. Grace as being is due to efficient causality, a causality that causes only a presence of immensity. But grace as grace, formally considered, flows from a new type of efficient causality, a new, specifically different type of efficient causality. So superior is this new type of efficient causality over the ordinary efficient causality that it results in a specifically new substantial presence of God, the presence that revelation describes as taking place at the divine inhabitation.[12] Since grace is a participation of the Divinity itself, an effect specifically different from the rest of created reality, the efficient causality that produces grace must be specifically different from that which produces the rest of being.

Nowhere, it seems, has revelation clearly taught that it is only within the limits of efficient causality that the theologian may seek for a further explanation of the problem of the mode of the divine indwelling. If it did, we would indeed be forced to seek for a new, a very new type of efficient causality. To explain a presence specifically different from the presence of immensity, we would need a specifically new and different type of efficiency, as Rétailleau states clearly. Precisely at this point, where he should explain the difference, however, Rétailleau seems to be weak.

Perhaps this theory can best be seen in its essential structure, and in its radical unacceptability, in the principle which lies at its foundation. Grace is a degree and a variety of being and as such it is produced by efficient causality and results in the presence of immensity. But under another aspect it is more than being. "It surpasses being; it is more representative of God than being."[13]

It is precisely from this "more" than being that Rétailleau constructs his theory. Since grace as grace, is more than being it does not seem impossible that by this "more" there is introduced a new relation founded on that new efficient causality, irreducible to the causality exercised in the production of being in general. This new relation would stem from the causality needed to produce the "more" and while it would be a relation founded on a type of efficient causality, since the causality is new, the relation would be new—the presence of the divine indwelling. Thus grace as being, since it is due only to the ordinary causality of efficiency, will give us only the ordinary presence of immensity. We must have some new causality operative to produce the new presence. This causality is precisely that required to produce the "more" than being that Rétailleau finds in grace formally considered as grace, that is, that by which graces surpasses being.

But what are we to make of the concept of that which surpasses being? Is it really possible to conceive of a being which surpasses being? This concept seems to represent an impossibility. On that ground alone we can find this theory unacceptable. However, even if we granted this concept, what proof is there that the "more" is necessarily due to efficient causality and not to another type of causality? Even granted that this more were due to efficient causality, what then is the intimate nature of this new efficient causality? It would seem that the efficient causality of God is not specifically different when he creates stones, horses, men or grace. The effect is certainly specifically different but not the type of causality at work. It would appear that Rétailleau's theory is left with the ordinary efficient causality that results in the presence of immensity. He is left with the same type of causality which Vasquez offered us to explain the divine indwelling, and which Rétailleau finds insufficient.

In conclusion we might say that both Galtier and Rétailleau justly emphasize the exemplary causality at work in the production of grace. But exemplary causality, joined to efficient causality in the production of any grade of created being, however high, does not specifically change the efficient causality involved. When a higher grade of being is produced we have a higher degree of the same causality and of the same presence—the presence of immensity.

The theory of the "new" efficient causality offers little chance of successfully explaining the mode of the divine indwelling. As Galtier presents it this theory has the merit of remaining at the threshold of the nature of this causality. The "more than being" theory of Rétailleau exposes the weakness of the metaphysics underlying this theory. Rétailleau, by attempting to develop Galtier's theory, has pointed up its insufficiencies. The very facts upon which Galtier lays such deserved stress, the sealing, the communication, the impression of the Divinity on the soul, cannot be explained by mere efficient causality.

It is important, however, that we appreciate the advances made by this theory over the objective theories discussed in the preceding chapter.

Both Galtier and Rétailleau have posed the problem more correctly than the objective theorists. The objective theorists have generally confounded the possession of God by acts of knowledge and love with the new presence which alone renders this possession possible. By failing to account for the new presence of God in the justified soul, the objective theorists destroyed the very foundation for the new possession which so preoccupied them. They conducted their investigations as though the knowledge of God, even experiential, could give to the soul the substance of the Divinity, really, substantially, newly present.

Galtier and Rétailleau, on the other hand, have posed the problem correctly. Revelation teaches two truths concerning the divine inhabitation. It teaches that the substance of God is made newly present. It also teaches that the just soul has a new capacity to possess the God so newly present. Nowhere outside of Galtier will one find the problem so clearly placed. He has taken us to the point where a metaphysical explanation may work most profitably and he has staked out the limits within which it may effectively speculate. His criticism of the objective theory has pointed up the difficulties any exponent of such a theory will have to answer. He has removed in advance for us the dangers of accepting certain incomplete solutions, by the way he has underscored certain of the data of revelation. These major contributions cannot be ignored even if the solution he offers is not accepted in detail. His solution appears to be unacceptable principally because the new type of causality invoked seems to remain exemplary causality, and this type of causality is not sufficient to account for a new substantial presence. Nor does it appear to account sufficiently for the supernaturality of grace itself, for it seems to leave us with grace as an imitation of the divine essense precisely as that essence is imitable in a creature and not as that essence is in itself.

What the theories of Galtier and his followers achieve in the ultimate analysis is a more perfect degree of participation for the soul possessing grace. This participation may indeed be visualized as a superhuman, superangelic degree of participation of the divine perfections. But the question remains: Does participation as such, strict participation, suffice to establish the soul as a principle of strictly supernatural acts? Does it suffice to deify the soul? The creature's participated perfection, whatever the sublimity of it, is still a participated perfection, an imitation of God precisely as imitable by a creature. Whereas the supernatural is specified by what is proper to God himself and not as he is imitable by creatures. That by which God transcends creatures is precisely inimitable by creatures. The creature, however noble its participated perfection, always corresponds to an imitability of the divine perfection and not to that perfection as it is in itself. It imitates God as he is imitable by creatures, and hence cannot be specifically supernatural, for the supernatural is specified by God as he is in himself, as he transcends creatures, as he is inimitable.

What must specify the created perfection as supernatural is not God as imitable by creatures but God as he is in himself. Grace must have some intrinsic reference to God as he is in himself and not merely as he is imitable by creatures. Participation, even raised to the highest degree, falls short of the supernaturality contained in grace. Could grace as participation be a fitting principle for supernatural acts?

Efficient causality does not then seem to explain supernaturality, nor involve a special presence of God. Adding the notion of exemplarity does not seem to help the situation very much, for in general any new perfection by which man participates God's perfection does not so evidently imply relativity to God as the Supernatural as it does to God Exemplar of all created and creatable imitations of his perfections. Certainly Galtier insists on God's immediate presence and sealing activity. But does he so explain grace, appealing to efficient and exemplary causality, that this immediate presence and activity on God's part is called for by grace? Is God's immediate presence not merely postulated? How is grace in this conception essentially relative to the Uncreated Gift? What in the soul corresponds to God as present not as Exemplar but as he in himself? What is the relation of grace to God as "Inhabitor"?

NOTES

[1] The works to consult are P. Galtier, *L'habitation en nous des trois personnes,* Roma, P.U.G., 1950 and *De SS. Trinitate in se et in nobis,* Paris, Beauchesne, 1933.
[2] The work to consult is M. Rétailleau, *La Sante Trinité dans les âmes justes,* Angers, Univ. Cath., 1932.
[3] Galtier, *L'habitation,* p. 208.

[4] *Ibid.*, p. 214.
[5] *Ibid.*, p. 218.
[6] *Item.*
[7] *Ibid.*, p. 219.
[8] *Item.*
[9] *Ibid.*, p. 234.
[10] *Ibid.*, p. 210.
[11] See Gonzales Ruiz, "La semejanza divina de la gracia, explicación de una inhabitación formalmente trinitaria," *Revista española de téologia*, VIII (1948), pp. 565-600; F. Joret, "Seigneur, où demeurez-vous?", *Vie Spirituelle*, XXVI (1931), pp. 13-26; T. Fitzgerald, *De inhabitatione Spiritus Sancti doctrina S. Th. Aq.*, Mundelein, Ill., 1949; Chambat, *Présence et union*, Ed. de Fontenelle, Abbaye S. Wandrille, 1945.
[12] M. Rétailleau, *op. cit.*, pp. 222 sqq.
[13] *Ibid.*, p. 224.

Chapter 7. The Theory of Scheeben

IN the nineteenth century the greatest theologian of the German language and the greatest theologian of his century, Matthias Joseph Scheeben, made a serious effort to investigate anew the patristic conception of
the divine indwelling, with its emphasis on the formal activity of the
Holy Spirit.[1] His theory was not easily come by, and it did not go
either unchallenged or undefended. In his earlier works, such as Nature
and Grace (1861) he by no means explained the divine inhabitation by
formal causality. In fact, he severely criticized the position that the
Holy Spirit was somehow directly and immediately applied to the soul
as some type of formal cause.

His original opinion was that although we can call God in some sense
a formal cause of our sanctification, it is not in the sense of an intrinsic,
inherent, formed and forming form, but in the sense of an extrinsic
exemplar-form, virtually containing the produced form, as a model can
be said to contain in its own superior way the perfection of the reality
which images or reflects it.

Supernatural spirituality surpasses natural spirituality for the former
expresses the distinctive features of the divine Exemplar. It is a work
specifically divine and is produced immediately by God. Scheeben here
rejects any third alternative between a formal inherent cause and an
extrinsic exemplar. God cannot be the first, so he must be the second,
if we accept the Fathers' statements about formal cause.

It is very instructive to read this early work of Scheeben and to note his approach to the causality operative in the divine inhabitation. Unable to deny the manifest testimony of the Fathers, he interprets them as describing a formal causality that is extrinsic and exemplary. The reason for this is the difficulty he sees in postulating any higher union. If one has an intrinsic formal cause then one has a limited forming cause, and a substantial union between the form and what it informs, with the result that God and the soul would then form one single substance. It was only after further study of the documents of tradition that Scheeben became convinced that the explanation he had given in *Nature and Grace* did not do justice to the statements of the Fathers.

It is also instructive to note that what caused Scheeben to change his position to one in favor of a more intrinsic formal causality was not a systematic presupposition, or a scholastic argument, but a triply thorough study of the data of revelation.

In his *Dogmatik* Scheeben explains what he calls two different, complementary, but by no means contradictory points of view concerning the mode of the divine inhabitation. The first theory we may, for the sake of convenience, call the scholastic theory; the second, the Greek theory.

In the scholastic theory the communication which God makes of himself to the soul consists formally and exclusively in the permanent influence which he exerts upon it, communicating to it created grace, and directing the works of the creature to himself as Object and End. It consists then on the one hand, of the production of grace in the creature, the production of a permanent perfection which bears a specific resemblance to the Creator. God thus draws the soul to an especially intimate union. He remains in the creature in a permanent manner, as long as the soul is free from grave sin, and he is there by a special title as the efficient and exemplary cause of this new perfection that is grace. This inhabitation is especially attributed to the Holy Spirit, for he represents divine love which communicates created grace, and is the model of that love in the creature which flows from grace. On the other hand, the divine inhabitation consists in this that God, by his grace, renders the creature capable of knowing and loving God as he is in himself. He offers himself to the soul as the object of enjoyment and of veneration, as an Object intimately present to the soul, as a final Object.

Both of these points of view of the scholastic theory rest upon the fact that God offers himself to the soul, gives himself lovingly to the soul in virtue of a right conceded by grace. The Holy Spirit realizes and represents, in the most real and complete fashion, that intimacy of life which human friendship seeks and which makes of the friends one heart, one soul, "one spirit".[2]

In contrast, though not in contradistinction to the scholastic theory, stands the Greek conception of the divine indwelling. This theory has been developed "in close connection with numerous texts of the New Testament", by Irenaeus, Athanasius, Basil and Cyril of Alexandria.[3] It considers the divine inhabitation of the Spirit as the most important constitutive element of the adoptive sonship conferred on man. For the inhabitation confers a participation of the divine nature, a union with God, a substantial cohesion with God. The Holy Spirit appears in this theory as a form which by its substance informs the soul to divinize it. Divine adopted sonship has thus the character of generation. It results from the communication of the divine substance by the generating principle.

The substantial unity, as it is spoken of by the Fathers, Scheeben declares at this point of his development, implies more than a similarity of substance in the generating principle and the adopted son. It implies also a "cohesion" of substances. This union of cohesion may be more or less strict. In its stricter sense it implies a true substantial union. But in the sense that we use it here it is less strict. In the less strict sense it can mean, for example, the union that exists between two independent substances, that are united to form part of an "organic" whole. As an example of this union Scheeben lists the union of natural father to natural son or also of husband to wife. This union may appear to be only moral, but it does have a physical basis. There is in some fashion a communication of substance involved. It could be called "organic".

When this substantial cohesion comes about from the fact that the substance of the one being is had by the second at least partially, as in the case of generation, we may call it a union of substances. Thus the Greek Fathers understood the "sharers of the divine nature" of St. Peter. It is a co-possession of the substance of the first being by both the beings involved in the union.[4]

Scheeben does not wish any such union of God and man as is had in the Incarnation. In comparison to a strict substantial union, the union of grace is like a moral union. But because it is a union of substances, not of wills alone, and because it arises from the communication of the divine substance to the soul, he prefers to call it a union of cohesion. Scheeben also uses the example of the marital union to express this union which is physical not moral, yet a union of cohesion between two independent substances.

The Holy Spirit thus dwells in the soul as if it were a form, as a quasi-form, of the soul itself. The divine gift, in view of which the creature may be called a god, deified, is a deiform quality produced efficiently by God and affecting the creature in which it is produced. This also consists in a mysterious union, for the substance of the Divinity fills the creature and informs it "in a certain fashion."[5]

The creature is the temple of the Spirit, his sanctuary, the holy dwelling place of the Holy of Holies. The sanctity of the adopted creature does not consist solely in a created quality but in a sealing, an unction. The creature is adorned, it is filled with the holiness of the Divinity, with the substance of the Divinity. There is a real relation between the soul and God like to that which exists between the soul and the body in the natural order. The creature's sanctity is in a sense also a substantial sanctity, for its formal cause is not a pure created accident. On the contrary, the formal cause is also a substance, a substance which the creature has truly appropriated—though only in an accidental way. The Holy Spirit presents himself in the soul, in virtue of this mysterious union, which is equivalently an information, as a grace which sanctifies the soul not only efficiently, but also formally.[6]

The substance of God, filling the creature, communicates to the creature something of the divinity's moral and physical force. Because of the creature's co-possession of his substance, God the Father envelops the creature in the love with which he loves the Son and gives to the creature the right to the glory and felicity of heaven. For the seal imprinted in the soul shows that this creature belongs to God in a special way, is intensely united to him and possesses already the first fruits of this love.

It would be insufficient to say that the Holy Spirit is merely a principle of life, acting from without upon the soul as the efficient cause of the vital force which he infuses into the soul. Rather he produces this effect as a principle belonging to the creature and somehow making a part of the creature's fullness of being. One can, in a certain sense, say that the creature is primarily living because he possesses the Holy Spirit. One can say that the Holy Spirit is the life of the just soul. But one would express this better, would better express the animation that takes place here, if he compared this animation not to "information" but to "coherence", to the coherence of a branch with the trunk, of the members with the head.

Scheeben insists much upon this notion of coherence, of substantial cohesion, and he insists that it is drawn from tradition. The Fathers, he says, place the strongest emphasis upon the fact that the Holy Spirit is not just an agent effecting the sealing from without, as it were, but is the Seal itself, creating its impression by its own self-donation, self-communication. The Holy Spirit is he who has sealed us ... The traditional point of view is also that the Holy Spirit is the ointment, the anointing and not merely the resultant odor. Again, Scheeben insists, the emphasis of tradition is not so much upon the agent as efficient cause, nor upon the effect produced, but upon the peculiar manner in which the effect is produced.[7]

Much emphasis is given also by Scheeben to the notion of spiritual seed. The Holy Spirit is given to us as a communication of the divine nature, as the process of generation gives to the son a communication of the substance of the father. There is some mysterious insertion of the divine nature into the human when the human person is adopted by grace, but there can be no confusion of the two natures. The Holy Spirit is a substance that is in some way poured into the creature to unite the creature to the Divinity. The union is somewhat like the union of body and soul where the soul is united to the body yet remains a subsistent form, capable of existing by itself when it is no longer united to the body as its form. The Holy Spirit plays the role of a form informing the soul. However, Scheeben adds, we are not to take this expression strictly, for the soul is not susceptible of being substantially informed nor can the Holy Spirit be the form of a creaturely composite. Nor can the human composite, already complete in the order of substance, receive another substantial information while remaining a human composite. Consequently it is impossible to speak of a strict information in this case. The Holy Spirit cannot enter into a matter-form relationship as the form. But there is a definite analogy between the matter-form relationship and the soul-Spirit relationship. There is an organic union between the two. There is no new substantial union. There is no third new nature. There is no confusion of natures. The Holy Spirit remains a distinct substance. But there is an organic union.

Scheeben seems to be torn between the desire for a union more intimate than a moral union and the fear of ending up with a substantial union. What he gives with the one hand he takes back with the other. On the one hand, impressed with what he is convinced is the patristic teaching, he wants the Holy Spirit to be more than an efficient cause of grace, and to be in some way a formal cause. A relationship analogous to that of form to matter exists between the Spirit and the soul. The Spirit does more than produce the created perfection of grace by efficient causality. His operation in the soul may be called an "equivalent information". It is analogous to the information of the body by the soul. The Holy Spirit may be called the soul of the soul. He may be said to inform by inhabiting. The union is "organic". The union resembles the hypostatic union. In the union of grace a superior substance attaches itself to an inferior substance so as to ennoble the inferior, fill it, penetrate it, while the inferior substance finds in the superior a perfection analogous to that which matter finds in form.

On the other hand Scheeben sees quite clearly that the two substances remain two, that there can be no substantial union, that the Holy Spirit cannot be an informing form.

In his effort to preserve both halves of the truth as he sees it Scheeben ends up with what is a mere moral union. The examples he uses of a jewel informing a box, of the union between father and son, show his indecision in formulating the type of union aimed at.[8] A certain organic union is had but it is the union of a perfume with its container. Evidently his long study of the Fathers had convinced Scheeben that a relationship analogous to form's relation to matter existed between the Holy Spirit and the soul, but he was unable to explain such a union in a way that would preserve the transcendence of God and avoid the philosophical difficulties involved.

Moreover he leaves very much in doubt what we are to conceive in his system as the relationship between created and Uncreated gifts. At times it looks as though created grace could almost be dispensed with. It is indeed a disposition that is fitting the soul to possess before the Holy Spirit comes, but it seems to be related to the Holy Spirit from a positive ordination of God, not from any intrinsic and necessary relation. If there be no metaphysical, intrinsic relation between grace and the Holy Spirit, then we might ask, where is the real change in man that corresponds to the new real relation he bears to God when he is justified?[9]

In the ultimate analysis what Scheeben appears to want is an information that is not quite an information, a quasi-information. The interest of his theory lies perhaps principally in the way he sets up the problem of quasi-information by the Holy Spirit. He comes extraordinarily close to the position of de la Taille, whose theory we shall discuss in the following chapter. De la Taille actually takes up where Scheeben left off.

NOTES

[1] Cf. Rondet, "La divinization du chrétien," *N.R.T.*, 1949, pp. 449-476, and 561-588.
[2] *Handbuch der katholischen Dogmatik,* Herder, Freiburg, 1925, III, pp. 359-361.
[3] *Ibid.,* pp. 363-364.
[4] *Ibid.,* pp. 364-365.
[5] *Ibid.,* p. 376.
[6] *Ibid.,* p. 376.
[7] *Ibid.,* pp. 371-372.
[8] *Ibid.,* p. 369.
[9] M. J. Donnelly has noted this deficiency in Scheeben's position, as well as Scheeben's tendency to a merely moral union. Cf. *Theological Studies,* VIII (1946), pp. 246-280.

Chapter 8.   De la Taille's Theory

THE apparent insufficiency of ordinary efficient causality to explain a new substantial presence and the insistence of the Fathers on the notions of "sealing", "anointing", and similar metaphors, turned the attention of theologians to another type of causality: formal causality. Two eminent theologians of the seventeenth century, Petavius and Thomassinus, had contented themselves with organizing the statements of the Fathers which pointed in this direction and had concluded that in some mysterious way the Holy Spirit gave himself to the just soul as its "form". But these theologians had left in the shadow the question of just how this was possible. What the connection might be between created and Uncreated grace, for example, was a question not explored by these authors. At times they so stressed the activity of the Holy Spirit in "sealing" himself upon the soul that they appeared to some extent to neglect the created gift of grace. In general they failed to establish any necessary connection between the created and the Uncreated gift, thus leaving the formal causality of the Holy Spirit hanging, as it were, in a void. At times it appeared that if the created gift could not be called superfluous, it was not more than a fitting disposition for the Uncreated. The sealing activity of the Holy Spirit seemed to be sufficient in itself to justify. Sanctifying grace in itself seemed to have little to do with man's justification.

Scheeben had in some ways pushed the investigation of formal causality farther. He excluded explicitly at least the imperfections that must not be attributed to the Holy Spirit if one were to call him a formal cause. He insisted that there could be no question of information in the strict sense. The soul is not capable of receiving a new substantial form constituting it according to its specific substantial perfection. It is already constituted according to its substantial perfection and is itself a substantial form, the substantial form of the body. Nor could God inform the soul in the strict sense of being the intrinsic principle of the soul's own specific perfection without the loss of either his own or the soul's identity. A mysterious quasi-information is as far as Scheeben's speculation led.

Galtier, on the other hand, developed the line of formal causality more in the direction of extrinsic, exemplary causality. Faced with the obvious difficulty that Scheeben had not answered, Galtier opted to interpret the Fathers as having meant an assimilation through extrinsic formal causality by their insistence upon sealing and anointing. God cannot be an intrinsic formal cause. If he were the distinction between Creator and graced-creature would disappear. Consequently, if there is to be formal causality, as the Fathers teach, it must be an extrinsic, an exemplary causality. Since exemplary causality is at work in all God's productive activity, how then does the production of grace differ from ordinary efficient causality? Galtier's solution is that in the case of grace it is, so to speak, that the image of God is deliberately sought by God as the efficient cause, while in other cases it is, so to speak, almost unintentional. That answer is perhaps weak, but then there comes a point where the mystery does not lend itself to further clarification.

One might indeed question whether the patristic images which Galtier so stresses actually do suggest an extrinsic causality. It is of the nature of an exemplary cause to achieve its effect through the medium of an agent. It is and it remains extrinsic to the effect. If it becomes intrinsic then it pertains rather to intrinsic formal causality. The metaphor of sealing, the insistence of the Fathers on immediacy, do not easily suggest an idea in an agent's mind. They do not so easily suggest extrinsic causality.

If the causality is extrinsic, exemplary, why does it effect so new a presence? Why does it bring about a presence so radically different from the presence effected by ordinary efficient causality? There does not seem to be much point in appealing to the nature of the term produced, grace, for the question is: Could such an effect as grace be produced by the efficient causality Galtier describes?

Rétailleau attempted to solve the dilemma in which the school of efficient-exemplary causality found itself by a theory according to which grace was not, as grace, produced by efficient causality. But if grace as grace is not produced by efficient causality, by what causality is it produced? To this question Rétailleau provides no satisfactory answer.

In 1928 and 1929 Maurice de la Taille reawakened interest in the dormant formal causality school by two articles of lasting interest. In the first, "Created Actuation by Uncreated Act",[1] de la Taille explains the divine indwelling by an appeal to the metaphysical concepts of act and potency. In the second article,[2] he replies to a flood of questions and objections that the first article had aroused. The theory presented in these two brief articles has continued to be debated until the present day and the criticisms of the eminent theologian's ideas have not diminished in vigor or in warmth.

De la Taille sees clearly enough that the theory of the divine inhabitation and of grace must be of a piece with a general theory of the supernatural as such. He develops his theory of the supernatural at length with regard to the case of the Incarnation.[3] He applies it also to the cases of the Beatific Vision and the divine indwelling, but less at length. The shortest possible formula for his general theory is given us by de la Taille himself: created actuation by Uncreated Act.

Applied to the case of the divine indwelling and grace this general theory results in the view of God acting as a quasi-formal cause with respect to the soul in the state of grace. Grace in the soul is actually the passive, created communication of the divine indwelling. When one has grace it is because one has God actually communicating himself to the soul in a fashion resembling the way a formal cause communicates its perfection to its effect. A formal cause exercises its causality, not by performing some action, but by its presence. Grace is not the consequent of the divine indwelling. Grace *is* the divine indwelling, viewed passively. It is the formal effect of God communicating himself by his presence in the sense of its being the very reception of that communication.

God is not a formal cause here in the strict sense, of course. He is not a form added to the soul, as a further modification of the soul. God and the soul remain distinct substances. The form which is added to the soul as a modification is grace. Grace is an accidental form which is newly actuated in the soul by the divine indwelling. It is a created actualization of an obediential potency of the soul. But its entire nature as a created accidental form consists in its being a modification of the soul by which the soul actually receives in a created, accidental way the substance of God thus present and communicating himself. God's presence therefore can be understood in terms of a quasi-formal causality. God, the Uncreated Act, by his presence, actuates the obediential potency of the soul to receive him. The actuation of this potency and grace are identical. Grace is the created actuation according to which the actuating Uncreated Act is received in created form. Between God, the Uncreated Act, and grace, his created reception, there is no intermediary. Grace is a formal modification of the soul. But as a formal modification, it is simply the actual reception of God communicating himself. Hence God communicating himself to the soul by grace must be understood as relating himself to the soul after the manner of a unique formal cause.

In plainer and less technical language, the meaning of de la Taille's theory is that God dwells within the soul in the state of grace in a fashion somewhat analogous to the way in which the soul dwells within the body. And just as the body lives by the life of the soul which animates it, so the soul in grace may be said to live by the life of God which animates and divinizes it. God is so intimately present to the soul in grace and the soul so shares in his divine life that it is permissible to say it is as if God were the soul of the human soul as analogously the human soul is the soul of the human body.

The difficulty with such plain language, of course, is that it is general and vague, and it does not explain how what it says is possible. Its meaning therefore can easily be misunderstood and distorted. That is one of the principal reasons why it is so necessary, in the ultimate analysis, to speak about grace and the divine indwelling in the technical language of a metaphysical theory. Such a theory aims to be as specific and as precise as possible. It attempts to obviate likely misunderstandings and distortions. And it aims to show how what it says is possible.

De la Taille's theory is a subtle one and it does not help our efforts to grasp it with regard to grace, in that he did not develop it with regard to grace so completely as he did with regard to the Incarnation. If it is possible to sustain it, it will certainly offer great advantages. It would be superior to any efficient causality theory so far seen in that it explains clearly a new presence due to grace. For if the mode of God's presence follows upon the mode of the application of his causality, we should certainly have in this theory a new presence.

De la Taille's theory would also have a ready advantage in explaining and not merely postulating the supernatural character of grace. For, granted that grace is a superior principle of activity, that it renders man capable of producing acts bearing a certain proportion to God as he is in himself, we have to explain, if we can, the why of this truth. We know from its effects that grace is supernatural, but do we ordinarily explain why or how? In de la Taille's theory, the supernatural character of grace would not only be inferred. It would also become somewhat comprehensible. For grace, as a created actuation of God himself, has a relativity to God in its whole nature that no natural creature could have.

This theory would also have a clear superiority to all exclusively objective theories of the divine inhabitation for it would explain the theological problem of the inhabitation without recourse to an "habitual" knowledge that precedes any acts. It would achieve an immediate union that is in no danger of being confused with the Beatific Vision. Nor certainly would one object to this theory, as some have objected to the objective theories, that the new presence of grace is only an intentional, psychological presence.

Let us now examine the theory in detail. In the following chapter we shall consider some of the objections strenuously urged against it by certain theologians.

Let us return to the formula expressive of de la Taille's general theory of the supernatural. Its direct application to the case of grace and the divine indwelling requires that the indwelling be understood in terms of a quasi-formal causality on the part of God. The formula declares that the supernatural—and therefore grace—can best be understood as "created actuation by Uncreated Act".

This formula and its application to grace and the divine indwelling cannot be understood correctly without some understanding of the meta-physical concepts of St. Thomas upon which they rely.

By act, de la Taille understands, with St. Thomas, the determining principle in a being, the principle which determines the being to a certain essential perfection or to an accidental perfection added to an essence. That which receives the perfection or act is called potency. Act and potency are correlative principles. Potency is ordered to act as a capacity of which act is the realization or fulfillment. The relation which act has to potency precisely as act, has nothing to do with efficient causality but is rather a union, a giving of itself to the potency. An agent or efficient cause will always be involved, acting to bring about the union, but the union itself does not afford an example of the exercise of efficient causality on the part of act with respect to potency.

A fundamental example of a potency-act relationship is the one of essence and existence. An essence like man, for example, can be considered a potency with respect to the act of existence which determines a man to be actually rather than merely potentially. The act of existence, of course, will reciprocally be affected by the potency in which it is received, with which it is united. It will be contracted within the limits of the essence. Potency functions as a limiting principle with respect to the act which it receives.

Another basic example of a potency-act relationship is that of matter and form. Matter is a potency for the act of form. Form gives matter specific determination. Matter can be either this or that kind of matter. It is this kind of matter rather than that depending on the substantial form it receives. Matter is the body of a brute animal or it is a human body, depending upon whether it has received a substantial form which communicates to it a strictly animal kind of existence, or a substantial form like the human soul, which communicates a human mode of existence to it. In either case, the substantial form received is in turn limited to the dimensions of the matter into which it is received. It will be the substantial form of this particular animal or human body which it informs. Matter as such (prime matter) never exists. It is simply potency. Only matter of a certain kind exists. But this requires that the potency of matter receive actualization by a substantial form which is related to it as act.

A third type of potency-act relationship is the one of substance and accident (accidental form). A man as a substance has the potency for many qualities, quantities, relations, activities, and so on. The actual qualities, quantities, relations and activities are accidents or accidental forms further modifying his substance. Thinking, walking, talking, for example, are actualizations or fulfillments of the potencies of his substance. They are related to his substance as act to potency. They determine the substance further with respect to its accidental perfection, and they in turn are contracted within the limits of the individual substance with which they are united. The substance analogically may be considered the matter and the accidents forms—accidental forms.

In God, of course, there is no composition of potency and act. God is Pure Act. He is Uncreated, Infinite Act. He is the "Uncreated Act" referred to in de la Taille's formula.

Against the background of an understanding of the relationship between potency and act in the composition of the being of creatures, the really significant term to be comprehended in the formula of de la Taille is "actuation".

Actuation may at first glance appear to be a third and unfamiliar element injected by de la Taille into the internal constitution of a being composed of potency and act. De la Taille tells us, however, that it is simply the union of the act with the potency, or the communication of the act to the potency, or correspondingly, the reception of the act by the potency. It is the perfecting of the potency by the act. It is a changing for the better, not of the act obviously, but of the potency. In all composition of act and potency the act actuates the potency. In the composition of matter and substantial form the form actuates the matter and is reciprocally limited and determined by the matter. In the composition of matter and substantial form the form actuates the essence. In the composition of substance and accident the accidental form actuates the substance in an accidental way.

When the animal form actuates the animal matter the actuation received is precisely the act which is giving itself, communicating itself to the matter. Act and actuation are identical. There is no strange third element. The form is received into the matter, is possessed by the matter. In a certain sense the form also depends on the matter which supports it. The information by the form is identical with the form informing. Form is information and act is actuation. There is no need to linger upon a discussion of the term actuation in such a case.

The consideration of matter and form and of essence and existence in a typical case like that of the animal, however, will not lead us very far in our investigation of the supernatural union of grace when it is to be understood as "created actuation by Uncreated Act". Let us rather consider the composition of man. In the human composite the soul has a special nature. It is spiritual and can exist apart from the body after death. Here then is a composite of matter and form whose nature is for our purpose considerably more interesting than that of the animal. The soul is the form, the act, the active actuator, so to speak. The potential principle is prime matter. There is a union of matter and form. A human composite is constituted. The human soul can exist by itself. Although it is the act of the body, it may yet continue to exist when the body corrupts. When it is actually informing the body, the soul communicates its existence to the body. At death it ceases to communicate that existence but continues to exist.

In other words we have here a case where actuation is not act. The information of the body by the soul ceases at death and yet the soul, the form, does not cease but continues in existence. The information, the actuation here, unlike the case of the animal, cannot be the form and the act identically. The matter-form actuation cannot be the matter-form act. At death the animation of the body, the informing of the body by the soul, the corporal life given by the form ceases, while the form continues on. The soul communicating itself is spiritual and incorruptible, while the communication received is corruptible. When the communicating principle is of such a nature that it can exist by itself, the communication of itself to a receptive potency will be different from the communicating principle itself. The communication will partake of the conditions of the receptive potency. We will then have an information which is not the form, a matter-form actuation which is not the act actuating. The information which is received will point to the form but it will not be identical with the form informing actively. The actuation will point to the act but it will not be the act.

Thus the case of the human soul offers to de la Taille his starting point to purify the concept of actuating before he applies it to God as a quasi-formal cause actuating the soul in the state of grace by his divine inhabitation. The only thing which interests de la Taille here is the fact that he finds in the case of the human soul a situation where actuation is not identical with act. But God could never be conceived as an act in every respect like the soul. Although the soul is an act which is not identical with its actuation, it is still in the position of receiving from the body which it actuates. While it is united to the body, it cannot exercise its functions integrally without the body. While it is united to the body it is dependent upon the body for its operations of thinking, willing, etc. Its position is not simply that of giving without receiving. The reunion of the body to the soul at the Resurrection will thus improve the condition of the soul. The soul is a co-principle of a composite. It bears an essential relation to the body. It is connaturally adapted and proportioned to a receptive potency and in this sense is limited, is dependent upon the body. Since such connatural proportion implies dependence, God could never be conceived as such an act, bearing such a relation to a receptive potency.

If actuation is not act, what then is it in the case of the human soul? A third ingredient entering into the composition of man? An intermediary between the soul and the body? According to de la Taille, even in this case, it is not a third ingredient. It is simply the union of the two, matter and form. It is the matter's being united to form. It is the matter's being actuated by soul. To say that matter is actuated is to say simply that matter has form, that matter possesses actuation. Soul is united to matter precisely by actuating matter. For soul to be a formal cause is for soul to unite itself, to give itself, to communicate itself, to actuate. Nothing intervenes between matter and form. The actuation does not intervene. The actuation is simply the possession of the form by the matter. It is the union of the two. It is the matter's being-informed.

De la Taille finds a parallel case in the situation that prevails in the Hypostatic Union, the union of the human and the divine in Jesus Christ. In that case there is an essence, the created essence, and there is the Uncreated existence of the Eternal Word, which is the actuating existence. But there is also a received existence, which is created, limited,

dependent. The actuating principle, the actuating existence is the existence proper to the Eternal Word. It is uncreated, sovereignly unlimited
and independent. But its received communication, its actuation, the
created existence, is limited by the conditions of the receptive potency,
the created human essence. There is no dependnce of the Uncreated
Existence upon the created human essence, for Uncreated Act gives
without receiving. It is on the active side, not on the receptive side. It
gives existence. It remains unchanged. It in no way depends upon the
created essence which depends on it for its existence.

Act here does not communicate itself by being identical with actuation.
The received existence, the received actuation is not the Act which is
actively actuating. The actuation depends upon the Act. It points to
the Act. It demands the Act that it be. It is unthinkable without the
Act, but it is not the Act. If, by an impossible supposition, we separated the actuation from the Act and gave the created essence only the
actuation, it would not become an individual being. For that one needs
an act of existence and not merely an actuation.

In the case of the Incarnation then we would have, according to de
la Taille, an existential Act, the Eternal Word, which is by no means
the actuation received, but which does actively actuate the created human
essence of Christ. Because the actuation is not identical with the Act
actuating (somewhat as in the human composite the form is not the
information) the actuating Act need be in no way limited, dependent,
receptive, contracted. On the other hand the received actuation, the
passive actuation will be limited, dependent, created.

The union remains immediate. Actuation is not an intermediate. It
depends upon Act. It cannot exist without Act. It is introduced as a
last disposition to Act, by Act. The person of Christ is one. There is
one Act of existence, the Eternal Word's uncreated Act of existence. But
there is also a received existence which is not Act. There is only one
Act of the one potency. Actuation, precisely because it is actuation and
not act does not exclude Act from the same individual being. It demands
Act. It clamors for Act and cannot be actuation apart from Act.

It is only in the case of the Incarnation that we have a case where
existential Act is not existential actuation. In the order of existential
composition in creatures, the act of existence is always identical with the

actuation. The existence of the human soul, for example, is precisely the existential actuation of the body. The one act of existence is actuation and act in the order of existential composition.

In the case of the beatifying union of the blessed in heaven with God, de la Taille finds another case of created actuation by Uncreated Act. Here God plays the role of form to the human intellect and the light of glory is the ultimate disposition or change for the better in the potency brought about by the form. The light of glory is the created actuation by Uncreated Act. It is not the Act. It is actuation which is not Act.

De la Taille thus builds his whole concept of the supernatural around the concept of actuation which is not Act.

The Uncreated Act can in no wise depend upon the creature. There will be no strict material causality upon the part of the creature and no strict formal causality upon the part of God. Rather the Act in question, God, will communicate Itself to the potency, and the potency will be perfected, bettered, changed. The change in the potency, the bettering will be the created actuation. This actuation, partaking of the conditions of the potency in which it is received, will be limited. It will be a passive actuation in the creature, dependent upon the creature, and depending for its existence upon the Uncreated Act absolutely.

When de la Taille declares that there will be no strict material causality and no strict formal causality involved in the case of the union of the creature with God, he does not intend to deny that there is formal causality involved on the part of God. But it is a formal causality which is only analogical to the ordinary formal causality of creatures. In God, the activity that corresponds to formal causality is free from the imperfections that necessarily accompany this causality when it is exercised by a creature. When the soul, for example, informs the body, we have information which is not the form. But the form truly informs. It is a true co-principle, connaturally proportioned to the body and limited by the body. The soul is somehow bettered by its union with the body, since it was naturally destined to union with the body. It gives life to the body, but it also receives support from the body.

If created actuation by Uncreated Act is possible, it will be without the imperfections involved in creaturely actuation. God will not be a formal cause. He will exert one of the functions of a formal cause but not the other. He will actuate without informing. He will not be bettered by the process. Where a created form, because it is created, can actuate only by informing, he will actuate without informing. Where the created form cannot give without at the same time receiving, he will actuate by giving without receiving.

When the Act is Infinite Act it is impossible that it receive, that it be supported, that it depend. The relationship of matter to form wherein the form receives support and limitation from the matter is clearly impossible in the case of God.[4] God will actuate the creature without suffering any of the limitations that a creaturely act must suffer in actuating a correlative potency.

For such an actuation as this one by God to take place, the created subject must be disposed, or changed for the better, elevated to receive the higher Form or Act. Thus whenever Uncreated Act wishes to actuate a creature, it will elevate, dispose and adapt the creature to receive Itself. This ultimate disposition will be the created communication, the created actuation, the bettering of the subject. Such an ultimate disposition will, as creaturely being, be produced efficiently by the entire Trinity. Considered in terms of formal causality, the disposition is the actuation. It is not the Act. It is a created actuation by the Act, disposing the subject to immediate union with the Act. It is union with the Act, passively considered. Grace, in this theory, will be a principle of being disposing the soul for immediate union with God.

Pure Act, in conferring Itself upon the soul, will be completely unchanged. It receives no bettering from the soul. It is absolutely unlimited and independent. It actuates. It does not inform. Of itself to actuate means to give, and the purer the act, the more purely it will give itself without receiving limitation or support. The only act which is absolutely Pure Act is God. He alone can give without in any way receiving. He alone can actuate without informing.

Thus in the production of grace God will actuate the potency of the soul to receive a perfection that is above its nature provided God wills and brings it about, the obediential potency of the soul in other words, and the actuation received, the communication made to the soul, will be grace. Grace, as passive actuation, will truly inhere as an accident in the soul. God as Actuator will not inhere but will be immediately united to the soul. His actuation, in other words, is not his efficient causality, with which he produces grace, but a sort of formal causality by which the soul's obediential potency receives its actuation by being united to its Act. Only in this case, the Act and the actuation are not identical. Grace and God are indissolubly linked.

Grace is radically supernatural for it is a transcendental respect to God as God is in himself, not only as he is imitable by creatures. As an ultimate disposition for the Act, grace is introduced by the quasi-formal causal activity of the Act and is unthinkable without the Act. What renders grace supernatural, and capable of the formal effects we ascribe to it, is not the fact that it is produced by the efficient causality of the Trinity, as every natural accident is, but the fact that it is created actuation of the Uncreated Act and thus sets man in immediate union with God as he is in himself. Grace is not merely some higher participation in the divine perfection, not merely even a superangelic accidental, absolute perfection. It is a supernatural accident. It gives the creature a proportion to God as he is in himself, because it is, of its whole essence, relative to God as he is in himself. This is what is meant by saying that it is a transcendent respect to God as God is in himself. Created actuation must, of its nature, if it be the actuation by Uncreated Act, be so constitutionally relative to God as he is in himself. Nothing could bear greater resemblance to Uncreated Act than its actuation, its communication. Grace, in this theory, is clearly gratuitous—no creature can have any exigency to actuation by God naturally.

Grace, in this theory, is intrinsically, constitutionally supernatural, and its supernaturality seems to be explained better than in any theory of mere participation, which while it may postulate the supernaturality of grace, arguing from the effects of grace, often does little more to explain this supernaturality than postulate it.

In de la Taille's theory the absolute accident, the positive accidental entity, of grace, will have, as any other accident, a relation to God as First exemplary and efficient cause. But—and to de la Taille this is fundamental—it will also have what natural accidents do not have, a relativity to God as he is in himself, to God as Actuator, as communicator of his own proper perfection. Grace as an absolute accident, as a positive, entitative quality, is totally relative to God as he is in himself. The whole being of grace bespeaks a relationship to God as communicating himself. Grace is what thomistic metaphysics refers to as a transcendental relation. More perfect supernaturality than this would be hard to secure for grace. Its whole being is as such a relationship to God as he is in himself, and as he is being communicated.

If grace be accepted as such a created actuation by Uncreated Act it is easy to see that a specifically new presence of God is had by the just soul. It possesses God himself as Actuator. The new union, looked at passively is grace. The divine inhabitation, looked at passively is grace, for grace is the created communication of God, grace is the union of God to man. Because there is this created communication of God to the just soul, the Uncreated Act, God himself, is "had", "possessed", by the soul in a new way. The just soul possesses God indeed, for it is actuated by God as Act—not substantially actuated by God, it is true, but accidentally actuated by God as Act. The union is accidental, but it is immediate.

God gives himself in this fashion, as Actuator, as quasi-formal cause, only to the just. The communication by which we possess God, is grace. It is grace by which we are enabled to possess the Divine Substance. The actualizing principle is God, the communication of the Principle is created grace. The relation between them is intrinsic. Both are necessary to explain the indwelling of God in the soul. The soul has God in a most perfect way because it is actuated by God himself.

It is important to see that for de la Taille the absolute accident of grace is a transcendental relation to God. With that understood one cannot claim that created grace is superfluous, as it may have seemed in certain other formal causality theories. Of course, de la Taille admits that grace, as created actuation, is also the foundation for a relation of union to God by intellect and will. It is not this relation that explains the supernaturality of grace, however, but the fact that grace is in its very being, according to its whole essence, a relation to God as Act. Man is supernaturally related to God by this transcendental relation. By this relation man is constituted united to God as Actuator. Grace does not "cause" the inhabitation except in the sense that is by grace, because man is perfectly disposed by grace, that man has the inhabitation. Grace is not given previously to the divine inhabitation.

De la Taille believes that by his theory he has solved a problem that has already faced those who inclined to maintain a solution to the problem of the divine indwelling on the lines of formal causality—he avoids a substantial union of the soul with God. For God is not a form informing the soul. That role is played by grace, which functions as a form. The substance of God is indeed communicated to the creature but in an accidental way. Grace is an accident. The union is a union of substances, and it is an immediate union, but it is an accidental union. The soul potency is actuated immediately and accidentally by the substance of God. The actuation is grace, and grace is an accident. The union of substances is therefore an accidental one. God the Actuator actuates the soul immediately however. Grace is no intermediary. What inheres is the actuation. What is possessed is the Act, God, the Divine Substance, in immediate union with the soul.

God and the just soul are united most intimately. Each of them possesses one and the same divine substance, the Divinity by identity and the soul by accidental actuation by this substance. God is participated by all creation. But he is possessed by, he communicates himself thus to the just soul, and only to the just soul. The soul possesses the Divine Actuator, not by being a co-principle of potency to it as co-principle of Act, but by being actuated by it. Because of grace's constitutional or transcendental relativity to God as he is in himself, grace is supernatural in a way no mere participation could be. Thus de la Taille feels that he has avoided the impasse at which every mere efficient causality arrives in trying to explain a new possession, a supernaturality for grace.

NOTES

[1] M. de la Taille, "Actuation créé par acte incréé," Recherches de Science Religieuse XVIII (1928), pp. 253-268.

[2] M. de la Taille, "Entretien amicale d'Eudoxe et de Palamède sur la grâce d'union," Revue Apologétique XLVIII (1929), pp. 5-26, 129-145. See also his "Théories Mystiques à propos d'un livre récent," Recherches de Science Religieuse XVIII (1928), pp. 297-325.

[3] The Schoolman, "The Incarnation" (Papers, Catholic Studies, Summer School, Cambridge, 1925), ed. by G. Lattey, Cambridge, Heffner and Sons, 1926.

[4] Wm. O'Connor, "A New Concept of Grace and the Supernatural" The American Ecclesiastical Review, 1938, p. 404.

Chapter 9. Objections and Replies

OBJECTIONS to the theory of de la Taille have been raised by a number of theologians. It is not possible here to consider all of them. We shall consider those which appear to be fairly significant and we shall attempt to answer them.

All the theological difficulties urged against de la Taille's position have been expressed in a general way in one author's conviction that it is in conflict with official documents of the teaching Church, traditionally repudiated by an almost unanimous majority of theologians, among them the greatest, and laboring under the gravest difficulties in itself and in its consequences.[1]

It has been maintained that de la Taille's theory is only a variation of the old theory of the information of the soul by the Holy Spirit—a theory long since frowned upon by the Council of Trent. The Council of Trent certainly declared that grace is the unique formal cause of our justification. But whether this need be interpreted as excluding created actuation by Uncreated Act is not perhaps as clear to all as it is to those who would urge the council's declaration as an objection to de la Taille's theory. Karl Rahner remarks that the Council of Trent's preoccupation was to establish beyond doubt the interior deification of man and to exclude a merely imputed justice.[2] Nowhere, he adds, does the council say that the interior grace in justification must be understood exclusively as created grace. Trent rejects a justice which would be merely imputed in an extrinsic fashion, with no internal form conferred, no real transformation of the creature. That was the issue at stake when Trent saw fit to make its statement. The least one can say in de la Taille's defense on this point is that it was not Trent's intention to settle the problem of how grace is caused, by what kind of causality grace arises in the soul.

The Council of Trent does speak of God as efficient cause of grace but that need in no way be taken as a contradiction of de la Taille's position, for de la Taille also holds that grace, as an absolute accident, is produced by the efficient causality of the entire Trinity.

Trent teaches that we are justified by an intrinsic form, grace, and that grace is the unique formal cause, that the form grace suffices, without any imputation of the justice of Christ, for the whole effect of justification. De la Taille's theory does not deny that. He holds that God is the efficient cause of justification and grace, of the accident grace coming to the soul. He merely denies that grace, or the deification of the soul, can be explained by efficient causality alone, since grace is of such a nature that it deifies man and brings with it the new substantial presence of God within the soul. According to de la Taille, such is the nature of grace that we are forced to postulate, over and above the efficient causality at work in its production, a quasi-formal causality on the part of God, that we may account for the wholly singular nature of the created quality grace. Trent would no more seem to pretend to say the last word on the causality of grace than it would pretend to have said the last word on the causality of the sacraments in calling them instrumental causes.

As a matter of fact, it seems that Trent rather suggests some type of formal causality when it refers to God as the efficient cause of grace and says he "seals and anoints" the soul. Galtier declares that the Council of Trent insinuates something more than the ordinary efficient causality since it refers to God as not only the efficient cause of his image, but teaches that we are sealed and anointed with the Holy Spirit, and grace, which is said to inhere in us, is also said to be poured out in our souls by the Holy Spirit. Galtier concludes that formal-exemplary causality is suggested as well as efficient.

De la Taille, far from denying the Tridentine doctrine, is intent upon complementing it. As common doctrine maintains that the Hypostatic

Union is produced by the efficient causality of the whole Trinity, without claiming thus to explain why only the Word is incarnate, so here the Council of Trent teaches that grace is efficiently produced by God as an interior form sufficient to explain by itself man's justification without extrinsically imputed justification. Other complicated questions which might arise with regard to the production of grace are not necessarily dealt with by Trent. If many theologians hold that the Person of the Divine Word actuates the sacred humanity so that there is in the humanity a real entity, a real foundation of the real relation to the Eternal Word exclusively, they do not thereby deny the efficient causality common to the entire Trinity in effecting the Hypostatic Union. The idea that Trent, by declaring grace a unique formal cause of justification, excludes de la Taille's theory seems unjustified.

It has been alleged that there is a clear opposition between the teaching of St. Thomas and the teaching of de la Taille on the question of grace and the divine indwelling. Aside from the customary difficulty one encounters in determining the position of St. Thomas on this controversial point, one finds nothing in citations so far adduced which would indicate such opposition. St. Thomas has said that we are rendered deiform by charity: that by charity we habitually love our neighbor; that in us there exists an habitual form inclining us to acts of charity; that our spiritual life flows from charity; that grace formally perfects the soul in its spiritual existence, etc., etc. How could any one imagine that de la Taille's theory would involve rejection of such formulae? It may be that de la Taille is in disconformity with St. Thomas. No citations from St. Thomas adduced to substantiate this opposition, however, give any clear indication that this is so. Even if it were so, of course, that would not mean that de la Taille was in error.

Certain difficulties that have been alleged as intrinsic to de la Taille's theory appear to be more forceful. It is maintained, for example, that de la Taille makes of God an intrinsic determining principle of the creature, and thus makes of God a strict form, informing the creature in the strictest sense. A vital principle gives to the activity which takes its origin from this principle its immanent being and specific character. For this, strict information is required. Vital activity issues from the visceral depths of the agent. Unless the vital principle of action is inviscerated in the agent by strict information, it is impossible for the activity to be vital, to issue from the depths of the agent. The vital principle must be intrinsic, in essential or organic composition with the agent. It must be the form informing by information in the strict sense. That is the line of argumentation often repeated by a theologian like Rétailleau. It seems to forget the necessity of recalling the analogical nature of our concepts as applied to God. Even when we speak of efficient causality in God we must free the concept of those imperfections it has when found in a created efficient cause. So here it would seem we could not a priori exclude the possibility of an actuation that is not strict information.

The argument continues that the actuation cannot serve as the principle of vital activity. It is a disposition which roots the vital form, Uncreated Act, in the soul, and as a disposition it is not responsible for the qualities of vital activity. If it is responsible we would have two forms, actuation and Act, pretending to actuate the same potency. This being impossible, we must choose: either grace as informing form, or the Uncreated Act informing by strict information.

Actually this difficulty will not be solved completely until man has resolved the mystery of man's cooperation with God in all salutary acts. But it may be said here that in de la Taille's theory the actuation belongs to the soul receiving it. It belongs to the man himself, and in acting through this actuation the man actually owns the acts produced. The Act, God, is in no sense a part of the human composition, nor does God make use of the actuation except as God makes use of the actuated-soul, instrumentally. The operations of the man in the supernatural order proceed from the soul of the man as that soul is supernaturalized by the actuation, grace, which is truly interior to the man. The supernaturalization of the soul has taken place through the active actuating on God's part, resulting in a passive actuation truly inhering in the soul, truly affecting the soul. The soul, modified by it, is then a principle of supernatural acts. The act is attributed to the man, as possessing this actuation inhering in the soul. Grace has been communicated to the being of the subject. In acting through this grace man is acting through his own soul as modified by this actuation. The act is attributed rightly to the man. The supernatural acts of man are truly vital for the form, grace, truly is rooted in man. They are vital since the form from which they proceed truly belongs to the individual man. The acts belong to the individual man acting.

Of the two forms proposed to us in the objection, one is really a quasi-form, God, which by no means informs. It actuates in an accidental way. Grace is a true form, passively received in the soul, intrinsic to the soul, inherent in the soul, modifying the soul. Grace is a form truly interior, inherent, communicated to the individual human being and consequently capable of modifying the acts of this individual human being. It is an accidental perfection of the subject. It inheres in the soul-subject as a form inheres. It perfects and modifies the soul. But it itself is the result of the presence of the Active Actuating Act, who confers it upon the soul, by actively actuating the obediential potency of the soul to this perfection.

The actuator in the case is God. The perfection is supernatural, since it stands as a transcendental regard to the Act, to God as he is in himself, conferring himself. The perfection conferred is a perfection of the soul. It is in the soul and of the soul, really intrinsic and inherent. Consequently the formal effects of grace may be predicated of grace. They may be predicated of the actuation.

But this by no means excludes the possibility of God's acting as quasi-form. Actuation involves the presence of the Act. Actuation is precisely unintelligible without the active Actuator. The formal effects of grace can still be predicated of grace as actuation, for grace as actuation confers all the perfection upon the subject that is normally conferred upon the subject by actuation that is act.

The Actuator is doing actively for the subject all that is done by the act of a natural accident. It is actuating a potency of the soul-substance. The act of a natural accident does this by inhering, by depending, by conferring itself upon the soul-substance through its identity with the actuation received by the soul-substance. In the case of grace, a supernatural accident, God the Act does the actuating, in the active sense, usually done by the inherent form, the form which is both act and actuation. But God does not actuate by inhering, by informing. He is distinct from the information which is the effect of his formal causality. Grace then is an actuation, not an act, but it remains an inherent form, conferring upon the subject the perfection usually conferred by an actuation which is also act, in the case of natural accidents. Since grace is actuation distinct from act, the difficulty of there being two acts, God and grace, is avoided. There is further no conflict when actuation is not act, for actuation, far from excluding Act looks to Act and demands Act that it be. Since actuation, which is not Act, is not Act, it does not exclude Act, but clamors for Act and is not possible without Act.

In so delicate and so complicated a problem as the divine inhabitation we cannot proceed by assuming that God's causality will follow the same pattern and be subject to the same limitations as a creaturely causality.

A friendly and appreciative critic, who would seem to wish to develop de la Taille's view in a way more radical than de la Taille's theory will permit, objects to a portion of the theory on purely philosophical grounds. It is not necessary for us to consider the technical metaphysical basis for his statement, but it is interesting to contemplate how far he is willing to go when he says, "... if the Uncreated Act chooses to communicate himself, he does, quite simply, communicate himself, and ... therefore the communication, being his self-gift, will necessarily and always be uncreated. How can self-communication of the infinite God be other than Uncreated?"[3] He is objecting to de la Taille's view of an actuation received in the potency through the formal causality of Uncreated Act. To him this implies limitation of the Act by potency, in spite of de la Taille's contention that created actuation distinct from the Act, if the former is received in the potency, is precisely what safeguards the independence of the Act. The objector sees no reason why, on the level of formal causality, God and the soul cannot be united without any actuation that has to be "received in" and so limited by a potency.

De la Taille would maintain that reception is the passive counterpart to the active communication of the form. If God communicates himself in some way, and he seems to, from the data of revelation, in grace, in the light of glory, and in the Hypostatic Union, then he would maintain there is a giving and a reception. But a reception, of course, would not mean a reception which implies dependence on the part of the Act. God would give, the soul would receive, a created communication distinct from the Act, yet possessing this communication, it would truly be said to have God, for the Act is inseparable from the actuation, which is a transcendental relation to God. God is not received and limited; the actuation is what would be received and limited. The Uncreated Act would actuate actively and the created actuation would be received and limited.

Here we meet the core of the objection. "How can self-communication of the infinite God be other than Uncreated?" The problem resolves itself into the concept of communication on which the objection is based. By communication it may well be that de la Taille means that state of affairs where two have the same thing in common. Then man and God would both have the Uncreated Act in common. In this sense, the Object, the Perfection, the Communicated, is Uncreated. But God would have this Act by identity, and man, in grace, by being accidentally actuated by the same Act. The Gift is Uncreated. The rooting of that Gift in the human essence would be through the created entity, grace, in the sense that he who has this accident is accidentally modified. Accidentally he is actuated by the Uncreated Act. Self-communication is certainly the gift of Self and the Self in question here is Uncreated. But the two who possess the communicated perfection need not possess it in the same fashion. If the Act, as passively communicated, were Uncreated, would there remain any interesting differences between God and man? An uncreated communication of an Uncreated Act would be, it would seem, an uncreated possession of an Uncreated Act. God possesses his Act in a fashion that is not created, contingent, finite. But man?

In the case of the Beatific Vision, it is true, the Object communicated is indeed uncreated. It is the essence of God. But there is room here to speak of a created communication also. The communication passively looked at, or the possession, is created. Is the possession by the creature of God's essence an uncreated possession? It begins in time, it is the possession of a creature and marked by the limitations of the power receiving it. Were this possession, this communication, uncreated, we would have uncreated possession of uncreated Act, which most theologians reserve for the one Being who is Pure Act, whose essence is his existence.

Where there is a giving there is a receiving. WHAT is given is most surely the infinite God. But the possession of God is not infinite and uncreated. He is had in a limited, created, finite way, a way that is capable of degrees and of growth. The Object communicated in the vision of God in heaven is uncreated. To say that the communication of that Object, the union of that Object with the soul or the intellect, the possession of that Object is also uncreated appears a very strange statement.

To make the communication intelligible, and to retain the distinction between man and God, we believe one must distinguish between the Object communicated, the Gift which is God, and the Act of communicating, an Act that belongs to God, and the passive communication, the way that Gift is had, the way it is possessed, the union of the Gift with the receiver. This passive communication must be created. A failure to distinguish between passive communication and the Gift which is communicated does not advance the theology of this difficult problem of how God can and does communicate himself.

The possession of God is not God except in the case of the infinite Being. If communication means the having in common of one thing, then man in grace has God, the divine Act, but in a very different way from the way in which God has it. Having in common does not mean that one must have the same object in the same way as the partner. If it did, God simply could not communicate himself. His self-gift, in the case of God is not his communication of that gift, unless one by communication means the Act of communicating rather than the communication passively looked at. And if one means the infinite Act of God, in what way is it communicated or had in common? In an identical, uncreated way? Then you have two Uncreated Acts, which is no small inconvenience.

It is not correct to assert that whenever a form is received in a potency there will be dependence of the actuating act. If God is capable of actuating a potency in a quasi-formal manner then it would be without dependence on God's part and yet the change in the potency, the bettering, indicates that something has been received in the potency. It does not prove that what is actively actuating is thereby dependent upon the potency. If God actuates the created essence of Christ, some change takes place in that essence. Surely it is not the same as it was before it was actuated by God. Does it follow that the Actuating Act, God, the Existence of the Eternal Word, is dependent?

The same author criticizes the idea of a substantial form giving itself in an accidental way in the theory of de la Taille. Since actuation is the communication of the self's act to the potency, if the form is substantial, it would seem that the communication must be substantial. "And if the act or form that gives itself is substantial, substantial too must be the communication or actuation."[4] Granted, if one admits no distinction between act and actuation.

De la Taille would reply that since the Gift and its communication are two different things, there would not seem to be any contradiction in asserting that the Uncreated Act, in itself substantial, gives itself in an accidental fashion in grace. The actuation that comes to the soul would be accidental. It can be absent. When it becomes present, it is present to a substance already substantially complete.

Although these philosophical objections do not invalidate de la Taille's theory, they do serve to point a finger at the weak spot in the analysis of de la Taille. It is unfortunate that de la Taille did not develop further the metaphysics of actuation in all the three cases he cites. Eventually it would seem to come down to the philosophy of formal causality and of the union of form to matter that would need further development before all the difficulties in de la Taille's theory could be ironed out satisfactorily.

The consideration of two more objections will afford us the opportunity to clarify further de la Taille's position.

The objection has been urged against de la Taille's theory that it implicitly denies the distinction between the natural and the supernatural orders.[5] De la Taille teaches that sanctifying grace is a created actuation produced in the human soul by God's own essence. This Act, God, is present in order that actuation may arise in the soul. Habitual or sanctifying grace is a reality informing its proper subject, man's soul. It is an actuation of the potency of the soul by the Act. "There is involved then, on the side of the potency or the created nature, material causality in the true sense, with regard to a supernatural entity; the natural is the true cause of the supernatural, this time in the order of accidents."[6] This implies a positive proportion between the essence of the soul as a thing of nature and the life of God. The soul, by its natural resources positively contributes to the essential constitution of a supernatural reality. But this destroys the gratuity of the supernatural.

This objection actually involves a fundamental misconception of de la Taille's position. To de la Taille the soul is an obediential potency in relation to the supernatural. An obediential potency is not at all like the ordinary potency of a nature for a perfection proportionate to that nature. The substantial perfection of the soul is not of the same order of perfection as grace and the Divine Indweller. Its substance is connatural with the rest of creation, not with God. The soul would be absolutely unresponsive to any creature which attempted to adapt it to be supernatural. It is responsive to God alone in being adapted to the supernatural. To be united to Uncreated Act it will require the intervention of God, disposing it to such union. It has no natural potency to such a union, and nowhere has de la Taille asserted that it has. Any agent other than God will find it impossible to dispose the soul to union with Uncreated Act. The soul as it is intellectual and is capable of becoming the subject of a spiritual accident has the requisite non-repugnance that is presupposed to God's omnipotence. But such non-repugnance by no means implies a proportion between the soul and the supernatural. Natural agents could work forever to dispose the soul to the supernatural and the effect would remain the same, an infinite disproportion between the soul and the supernatural. The unique agent capable of disposing the soul to the supernatural remains God, for only to God will the soul respond obediently. An obediential potency simply refers to the fact that a being is of such a nature that it would not be impossible for it to receive a modification or actuation that is above its natural capacities, provided God will it and actuate it.

Grace is the divinely infused ultimate disposition that disposes the soul for the Uncreated Act. With grace the soul is no longer undisposed, as it is also no longer a mere natural soul. It has been elevated. The accident, grace, is not another natural disposition. It is not either the Uncreated Act, but it is a disposition received in the soul, rendering the soul accidentally connatural to God as he is in himself, uniting the soul to the Uncreated Act. The substance of God and the substance of man are accidentally united, because man possesses accidentally, the Divine Substance. The two have in common that which is proper to God, but God has it by identity and man has it by being accidentally actuated by it.

De la Taille thus maintains no positive proportion between the natural soul and the supernatural. Quite the contrary. With unmistakable clarity, he declares: "The Uncreated Act can in no way depend upon any creature. It will give itself and receive nothing. Thus, on the part of the creature there will be no material causality and consequently on the part of the Act no formal causality properly so-called."[7]

The final objection which we shall consider is the one which maintains that in de la Taille's theory grace is the consequent of the divine indwelling and not as "traditional theology and most notably the thomist tradition teaches" the principle of the indwelling. "Note de la Taille's confusion. The thing principled—the indwelling—causes its own principle."[8]

The "confusion" of de la Taille is perhaps less evident than it seems. In the theory of de la Taille it is not accurate to say that grace causes the divine indwelling, for the passive actuation, the communication, is the divine indwelling passively looked at. And grace is not the cause of itself. Neither does one find anywhere in de la Taille the suggestion that grace causes the Active Indweller, who is God. Nor can one say that in de la Taille the indwelling or inhabitation is the thing principled, nor is it the cause of grace. Grace is not the consequent of the indwelling, for grace is the indwelling, viewed passively. It is the effect of God communicating himself, it is the communication received.

It is alleged in the objection that traditional theology teaches that grace is the principle of the indwelling. Certainly de la Taille would maintain that the indwelling is had because grace is had. Grace is what makes the difference between having the divine indwelling and not having it. It is thus "through" grace that one has God indwelling. When one has grace one has God communicating himself. One has the passive communication, for grace is the passive communication. De la Taille would also be able to say that it is by means of grace that God is constituted newly present and newly possessed, but he does not maintain that grace is the principle of the indwelling in the sense of its being causally prior to the divine inhabitation.

It would not be an easy task, in any case, to establish that "traditional theology" has maintained such a causal priority for grace, if by traditional theology one means a morally unanimous consent of theologians. Certainly this is by no means clear in the case of the Greek Fathers, who may be considered representative of traditional theology.

What is the relevancy of these criticisms which we have presented in this chapter?

It does not appear demonstrable that de la Taille's theory is in any way opposed to the position of Trent on the causality of grace. His position appears also to be most consonant with the many texts from the Greek Fathers that would suggest some type of formal causality, and perhaps more than an extrinsic formal causality, in the production of grace. On the other hand the difficulties or the obscurities of the theory in the speculative order cannot be minimized. Principal among these obscurities is the very concept of actuation. De la Taille would have done his admirers a distinct service if he had dealt more at length with this concept as it is verifiable in each of the three cases of the supernatural. The implications of this concept to the treatise on grace as a whole need to be worked out in more detail before a satisfactory evaluation of the theory could be given.

Concerning the term actuation, de la Taille tells us that he finds it convenient because it allows him to class in one genus and under one descriptive term diverse realities where there is given a possession of the divine by the creature, where there is a receptive capacity which is actuated by God, and where there is more than the Uncreated Act to be accounted for.[9] He tells us that the actuation is the communication of the act to the potency or the reception of the act into the potency (where the act is not God), it is a perfecting of the potency by the act. Union of potency with act or actuation of potency by act is the same thing.[10]

In the three cases of supernatural actuation by Uncreated Act the actuation received is a reality distinct from the Act. But also in the case of the human soul the received information is not the same reality as the soul informing. In the existential line, man has the human essence and the received actuation which is identically the act actuating. The existence is the act by which the man exists. But what of the composition of matter and form in man? Here, in the line of matter-form composition, the actuation is not the act, the information is not the form. Hence we do seem to have three essential principles in man: prime matter, form, and the received information which is not form. To which, doubtless de la Taille would reply that we have not only two principles of being but we have their union, and that is all he is saying. Union of potency with act or actuation of potency by act is the same thing. Nevertheless de la Taille's theory when it is applied to the human composite seems to leave the reader unsatisfied. Perhaps this is due to the fact that the human composite is a rather unusual composite.

It would be most interesting to see a complete analysis of the three situations where de la Taille's theory has been applied to the supernatural worked out in detail. Until that is done the theory exerts a certain appeal but leaves one with a sense of incompleteness.

NOTES

1 Rétailleau, op. cit., p. 107.
2 Rahner, op. cit., p. 155.
3 P. J. Kenny, "Created Actuation by Uncreated Act," Australian Catholic Record, XXVII (1950), pp. 215-216.
4 Kenny, art. cit., p. 219.
5 See T. U. Mullaney, O.P., "De la Taille vs. Thomistic Tradition," The Thomist, XVII (1954), pp. 1-42.
6 Mullaney, art. cit., p. 22.
7 De la Taille, "Actuation," p. 254.
8 Mullaney, art. cit., p. 23.
9 De la Taille, "Entretien," p. 134.
10 De la Taille, "Actuation," p. 253.

Chapter 10. The Value of de la Taille's Theory

IN the final analysis, despite its obscurities, it is the theory of de la Taille which seems the most solid and the most enlightening theory of the divine indwelling. It assures a presence which is essentially new and yet which is substantial, not merely psychological. There is no problem about baptized infants in this theory. It gives a metaphysical foundation for a new possession that is a real possession.

It assures a radical supernaturality to grace in a way no other theory does and it does this by rendering grace more intelligible. It does not, as some theories do, merely postulate the supernaturality of grace while leaving no metaphysical possibility that grace be so supernatural. It forms the sole adequate basis for an objective communion of the soul with God in knowledge and love.

If the theory can also be applied to the Beatific Vision and the Hypostatic Union, then it will offer to us a unified approach to the whole structure of supernatural reality. This theory also has interesting and illuminating reflections to shed on the nature of meritorious activity. It also unifies and renders more intelligible the formal effects usually ascribed to grace.

In de la Taille's theory all the effects of grace are centered around and explained by this one concept of grace as created actuation by Un-created Act. For, in this theory, whatever is a formal effect of grace will be a quasi-formal effect of the Uncreated Act impressing itself upon the soul. Thus the radical supernaturality of grace and its effects as sharing in the divine nature, adoptive sonship, and its effects as remissive of sin all receive a new focus when they are read in the light of the theory that grace is created actuation by Uncreated Act.

Precisely because of the way that grace is produced according to this theory, because of the way it arises in the soul, grace will assimilate the just soul to that grade of intellectuality, spirituality and life which is proper to God alone. It will do this infallibly and necessarily. This is due to the fact that it is produced not only by God's efficient causality but also his quasi-formal causality. By nature man was an image of God's intellectuality. Hence he was capable of possessing God as he is found in his creatures, in his similitudes. But by grace he will become a new image of God, as the Greek Fathers so often repeat. He will become newly capable of God, this time capable of God in a fashion like to God himself. This is due precisely to the fact that the proper effect of a formal cause is to assimilate the effect to the proper perfection of the cause itself, and not to some likeness of the cause.

The formal cause communicates. That is its proper note. It communicates its own perfection to the material cause. It assimilates it formally to itself. Thus the soul communicates its perfection to the body and the body is a sentient, thinking body. It is precisely in the way that it causes that a formal cause differs from an efficient cause. An efficient cause by its action produces an effect that imitates, in a similitude, the perfection of the cause. The efficient cause does not communicate that perfection which is proper to itself. It produces an effect which is a participation of its perfection by a similitude. In de la Taille's theory the divine substance in its own proper reality is immediately applied to the soul as a quasi-formal cause. De la Taille's theory appears to be nothing more than a transcription in terms of metaphysics, of all the images of the Greek Fathers on sealing, impressing, anointing, and so on.

Precisely because of this type of causality, a quasi-formal causality, the union of God the Actuator and the soul as subjective potency, is formally assimilative. Quasi-formal causality assimilates the soul to the proper perfection of God. It renders the soul a sharer in the divine nature. The soul is assimilated to the intellectuality which is proper to God as he is in himself. It is capable, radically, of knowing God as God knows himself and possesses himself.

It is difficult to see how any theory that ascribes the production of grace exclusively to efficient causality can so explain the supernaturality of grace. Every theory will of course postulate such a sharing of the divine nature. Revelation requires it. But it does not appear that any theory of exclusive efficient causality can render this sharing of the divine nature intelligible.

In de la Taille's theory the soul, newly assimilated to the divine perfection, the divine spirituality, accidentally modified in its essence, is truly capable of knowing God as God knows himself. The soul is truly deified. It is lifted to a grade of intellectuality where it is connatural, though undue, to the soul to see the Uncreated Divine Essence —intuitively.

The soul with this actuation has the root capacity for this act of vision. It is formally capable, given proper development of its natural faculties, of loving God as God loves himself. This is where de la Taille's theory rejoins the objective theories on a vastly superior plane, on a plane that offers the conditions of the possibility for a true objective union. For there have been some objective theorists who have wished to maintain an actuation of the intellect while denying any actuation of the essence of the soul such as de la Taille has.[1]

The fear that retains some theologians from admitting an actuation of the being of the soul is the apprehension that such an actuation involves a hypostatic union, with the divine Act of Existence replacing the human act of individual existence. The whole point of de la Taille's distinction between actuation and act appears here. In no sense does God the Actuator become the act of existence of the graced soul. Actuation is not Act. It is created, Act is uncreated. It begins in time, God is eternal. It may cease if the subject sins gravely. It is an accidental actuation, not a substantial actuation. It is a disposition to the Act, introduced by the Act. It is the changing for the better that renders the higher form admissible. But it is not the Uncreated Act Itself. In no sense does the soul become a confusion of human and divine or lose its act of existence to assume the divine existence.

Moreover the theory of de la Taille supplies the basis for an objective union that is more than ideal or psychological. The theory is not set forth explicitly in St. Thomas, but the metaphysics presupposed by de la Taille is thomistic. The metaphysical principle is that the mode of being of the subject must be proportioned and adapted in such wise as to prepare the faculty for the specific type of operations to which the faculty is destined. Thus for there to be an actuation of intellect, inchoatively, and an actuation of will, it would seem that there must be a prior actuation of the essence of the soul. The active potency must be commensurate to the concrete essence of the acting subject. The essence is elevated that the potencies may be elevated. It is the subject, properly speaking, which acts through its faculties of intellect and will, and were the faculties elevated without the subject's being elevated, the act could hardly be said fully to belong to the subject.

A created faculty could not so elevate the subject were it divorced from Uncreated Act. Neither could a created gift of grace, considered as arising by exclusively efficient causality. There is an infinite disproportion between the excellence of participated similitude and the excellence of Uncreated perfection. In the de la Taille theory there is no danger of isolating created grace in such a fashion that it appears an entity so proper to the subject, the soul, as to scarcely be the grace of Christ. Created grace incessantly depends upon the justice of Christ incessantly acting upon us. It is always an actual sharing in the sanctity of Christ. We are just as members of Christ and the reality of created grace would be falsified and endangered in fact by a theory which considers it as a reality that is autonomous and separated from the grace of Christ, the justice of Christ. Our good works, done in grace, were grace so separate, would by no means efficaciously proportion us to the Beatific Vision. But no such separation is had. It is the Spirit of Christ who acts within us. Our justice finds roots in Christ. It is inserted in him. It is not inconceivable, however, that this truth could be obscured by theories which, refusing any quasi-formal causality in the production of grace, betray an immanent tendency to ascribe its supernatural effects to grace in such a fashion that the created gift, a produced quality, seems to produce these effects almost as a separate, independent, autonomous reality. Such a tendency is clearly absent from de la Taille's position.

If we grant this actuation of the essence of the soul, then all the truth in the objective theory would seem to be rendered intelligible. A genuine objective union that is more than psychological becomes for the first time really possible. Without this actuation, the objective possession seems the possession of an image.

Let us develop a little further the question of objective actuation as it is made possible on the basis of de la Taille's view of the actuation of the soul. De la Taille always discusses such an actuation of the intellect in relation to the Beatific Vision but his thought can legitimately be prolonged.

We might maintain in this life an actuation of the will by Uncreated Act, and, also in this life, in a restricted sense, an inchoative actuation of the intellect by Uncreated Act—always presupposing the prior actuation of the soul.

If in fact, we consider the nature of man's supernatural meritorious activity, it seems that such activity would presuppose an actuation of the will by Uncreated Act. For the supernatural activity of man's will is destined to merit for him eternal life, the life that is proper to God himself. It is destined to merit for him a life that is proper to God alone, a life transcending all of man's natural powers, exigencies and efficacious desires.

In the Beatific Vision God will become immanent to the human spirit. There will be an objective identity of subject and Object. Man will be rendered objectively God, in the sense that the Object, God, chooses to identify himself with the knowing subject, not according to the subject's form of existence but according to his intelligence. Here on earth man possesses that vision in germ, inchoatively. Hence here on earth man must be disposed, in a permanent fashion, to tend by his will-activity to this vision. He must be capable of meriting it by acts which belong to himself, are properly his own acts, flowing from a principle intrinsic to himself and really possessed by him.

This vision is a good not only transcending man's natural powers but transcending all created powers of any kind. It is a good proper to God as God is in himself. If man is to have an efficacious orientation to such a good, the created will that is to merit must be so united to the divine Act that it may truly be said to appropriate the transcendent virtue of the divine Act to whom this vision is proper. The will is the proximate principle in man that is to merit this transcendent good. That this proximate principle be efficaciously orientated to this transcendent good and be the principle of merit of that good by its own acts, it requires a real union with the Agent in Act proportioned to acts efficacious of the vision.

That man's act be truly meritorious of the divine good of eternal life the first thing required is that the act be in a true sense the act of the man himself. It must proceed from man as the subject. But it must proceed from the subject as supernaturally meritorious. That such a transcendent effect proceed from the human will, it appears that it must first be really united to the transcendent Agent who can proportion it to this effect by constituting with the will a complete principle of the act.

In de la Taille's theory the reality of grace is an actuation, is inseparable conceptually from the Actuator, is a transcendental relation to God. Precisely because it is an actuation, created grace elevates the remote principle of merit, the soul. It seems consistent to suppose that the proximate principle, the will, appropriates in a mysterious fashion the divine Act that is immediately united to the soul when the created actuation of grace is present. Were created grace produced exclusively by efficient causality it could not proportion the remote principle to God as he is in himself. No creature, viewed in its own reality, can do this. But as actuation, grace is essentially relative. It is relative in all its reality. It is a transcendental relation. It requires Act. It implies Act. It is had because Act is possessed in its substantial reality, and possessed immediately. Hence the human will is in the position of being able to appropriate the virtue of this Uncreated Act which is communicated to the soul. The Uncreated Power and Virtue of God gives itself to the human will and the human will is elevated. The will of the human subject is thus amplified in a divine direction by a transcendent force, a created actuation of the Uncreated Act. It appropriates the divine force, enriching its native force with a superior power, divinizing its own activity by a communicated, not participated, divine reality, the Uncreated Virtue of the Divinity.

In this case we may truly speak of a possession that is more than psychological. The actuation of the will, which is created, implies not only a communication on the part of the Act, but a possession of that Uncreated Act, as communicated, by the subject's will. There will be a real though mysterious appropriation in activity of the divine force by the human will. God will act, in meritorious activity, through the human subject, which is elevated by an intrinsic actuation of the soul. From the actuated soul there emanates a will itself actuated by the divine force. This is the true significance of the real possession that the objective theory has in vain attempted to establish on its own terms. It is no mere psychological possession.

The objective theory has insisted greatly upon the role of knowledge in the objective union. Is it possible that this aspect of the objective theory can be rescued and placed on a secure metaphysical basis, on a basis that would not appeal to a nebulous habitual knowledge, never actualized, which is supposed to assure a real presence?

It would seem that this is quite possible.. We can maintain an inchoative actuation of the intellect in faith. We are speaking here of formed faith, faith in the pregnant sense so often employed by St. Paul. We are speaking of faith animated by charity, faith as initial justice, the faith which is the fountainhead and support of the life of the just. We are not speaking of a mere theoretical assent to a speculative proposition but of a complex act solidary to the whole man's surrender to God, involving his heart, engaging his will, implying a submission of his whole being.

No inchoation of the transcendent goal is had without grace. An inchoation involves a positive disposition. A positive disposition involves at least actual grace. There is no commencement of the vision without a communication of grace and if this grace is transient, the communion will be, on the plane of inchoative actuation, a transient preparation for this actuation. It will not be an actuation in the true sense, even inchoatively, for eternal life. The full actuation is God himself offering himself freely for our enjoyment. An inchoation of that is always an inchoation of God's giving of himself in his full reality.

In a restricted sense one can speak of an actuation of the just soul by the virtue of faith. Grace in the just soul is truly an inchoation of the divine life and not merely a title to such life. It is a real commencement of it. Even prior to any activity, and here the objective theory is correct, grace in the infant is a commencement of the life of glory. Insofar then as the intellect is an appetite for truth, perfected by the virtue of faith, it can be said to be inchoatively actuated by the Uncreated Act. It can be said to be in tendency to the full actuation of the Beatific Vision. The intellect is thus finalized by God as he is in himself. Vision is anticipated by faith as the end is anticipated by the finalized nature. For this intellect is the intellect of a subject efficaciously disposed to the transcendent end.

The assent of faith in the just man would then be not only a conceptual assent but an assent of communion with God communicating himself in his plenary reality to the just soul, and drawing the believing mind towards a fuller communion in the ineffable union of the Beatific Vision, where the mind will be actuated by God in such wise as to become objectively God. But the intellect in this formed faith would not be actually united to God acting as immediate Actuator. That is reserved for the vision of God in heaven. The intellect rather would tend actively to such an active union, drawn by the touches of the interior Regent and Master actively communicating himself to the soul. It is God, in his proper reality present to the just soul, that is drawing the intelligence to the full communication that he has set up for it in the Kingdom of his love. If the intellect in faith aspires, if it is in tendency, if it actively seeks and desires this union, it is that God has already given himself to the soul and has begun here the communication he will complete in heaven to the intellect. But there is already a real communion of the intellect and God, for the just soul obscurely perceives the invitation of God to full union, an invitation that is reflected in the soul's sentiment, direct, not reflex, of God's presence—for God is present, actuating the just soul and the just will.

Thus with the development of the habit of faith and its dominion over the activity of the subject the intellect will submit more and more and lovingly to the touches of the interior Regent and Master, preparing itself more and more completely for the actual union of vision, the complete actuation, realizing ever more completely the tendency divinely implanted with faith, actualizing its proper finality as an appetite, inchoatively. The ultimate end will deploy more and more the motive force that it possesses in the interior of the intelligence finalized toward it until the dawn of the celestial vision breaks, now no heterogeneous transformation but the fulfillment of the actuation inchoate from the beginning in the intellect of the just.

In the theory of de la Taille it is created grace that is the metaphysical foundation for an objective union through knowledge and love—but created grace as actuation, not, conceivably, as the effect merely of efficient causality. Just as grace as actuation is the foundation of the new relationship to God which we call the divine indwelling, created grace is the unique, intrinsic, inherent formal cause of this new relationship. Created grace by itself alone suffices to explain this new relationship and no second intrinsic formal cause is needed. But the very reason why created grace is capable of so explaining the new relationship and founding an objective union and presence that is real is because created grace is actuation and can never be divorced from the Uncreated Act whose created communication it is. Only because it arises in the soul by God's quasi-formal causality can grace have such extraordinary effects, transcending the whole world of created agents.

Without the quasi-formal causality of the Uncreated Act, created grace simply does not seem capable of explaining such a new relationship as the divine inhabitation involves. Such radical supernaturality as revelation ascribes to grace seems inconceivable if we depend upon efficient causality for an explanation. As a positive entity, founding a relation of union, grace is a creature as any other creature and refers us to God as Creator, imitates God as he is imitable by creatures, gives us a share of divine perfection in a similitude—but does it do anything beyond that? If we postulate that it does, and we must, do we still leave open the ontological possibility of the fact we postulate? If created grace is produced by exclusively efficient causality it too will be a likeness or similitude, glorious no doubt, but a similitude that will assimilate us to God as imitable by creatures, not to God as he is in himself.

To de la Taille, created grace and Uncreated Grace are absolutely inseparable, and not merely by postulate. Created grace is by no means dispensable, as it seems to be in some older formal causality theories. An ultimate disposition is not separable from the form. Nowhere is the connection between created grace and Uncreated Grace so luminous as in de la Taille.

In his theory it is not possible to fall into a way of speaking—much less of thinking—in which the divine indwelling is described as if it were consequent to the production of created grace, thus leaving the entitative supernaturality of grace hanging in a metaphysical void. If the divine indwelling is not prior as form, what becomes of the supernatural character of grace? Any efficient causality theory does not appear to be able to answer this question. De la Taille's theory on the other hand, seems most illuminating. Grace is precisely the created communication of the divine substance to the soul. The just man has the divine substance by grace, in common with God. The just man has it accidentally, gratuitously for he is actuated in an accidental fashion by God. God possesses it by identity of nature.

It is easy to see that in de la Taille's theory the just man is interiorly holy. For he is drawn to God in an entirely new way, set apart from creatures in an entirely new way. He is actuated by God. Grace, as actuation, is formally unitive.

Ordinary theories of grace conceive God as the term of a new relation in the divine indwelling—as the efficient cause of grace. In this conception the divine indwelling seems to be purely a term of a relationship, with God only extrinsically connoted, as is the term of every ordinary relation—for in such a relation the cause does not enter into the definition of the related being. De la Taille's theory has grace related essentially to God. It is a transcendental respect to God. God is not simply a term extrinsically connoted. Grace is unthinkable without the Actuator who is causing it. An actuation is unthinkable without an Act.

In de la Taille's theory it is also clearly explained why we are called and are friends of God, for whatever is required that a man be capable of benevolent love of God is given to him with grace. The graced soul possesses the Beloved's very substance in an accidental, gratuitous fashion. He is orientated to God efficaciously and through grace he is able to love God as God loves himself. Indeed, if we may use the term, he is able to love God as "another self", for God's loving initiative has raised him to such a communion, by actuating him through created grace, that he shares the very goods of God.

The just soul is not, however, only a friend of God. He is called and in truth he is the adopted son of God. We must note here the superiority of the de la Taille theory in explaining this formal effect of grace. As we saw of the the new relationship to the divinity which we call the divine indwelling or inhabitation, by grace man has an accidental possession of the divine substance. For man is now accidentally referred to God by this actuation in a way similar to the mode in which the Eternal Son and Image is referred, of his whole reality, to the Father.

Created grace, by reason of the way it arises in the soul, imprints in man relationship to God, a new image of God's intellectuality. By the very fact that grace is given as created actuation man is a sharer in the divine nature and bears a new relationship to God as he is in himself. And this is the result of the very process that creates grace. Because of the way his grace proceeds from God, man images the nature of the Godhead, somewhat as the Son images the nature of the Father according to the way that he proceeds from him. Similarity of nature resultant from the origin of grace and identity of nature and a relation of origin, both essentially relative, these are the two terms of comparison in the idea of Sonship. Again it is grace that is the unique, intrinsic, inherent, formal cause of this sonship. Again grace is such only because of the way it arises in the soul, through the quasi-formal causality of God, because as actuation it is inseparable from the divine Actuator.

In de la Taille's theory grace would be remissive of sin by its own physical reality and without any added divine positive ordination. Grace would remit sin by metaphysical necessity, for grace is nothing else than God's communication of himself to the soul.

In conclusion we might say that it is obvious that all of de la Taille's structure is founded on the ontological and not on the psychological plane. He insists upon founding ontologically the new presence of God, his substantial presence, contemporaneously to the infusion of grace. He safeguards the ontological aspect that is so well underscored by Galtier and the efficient-exemplary school of thought. He avoids any danger of finishing with a merely representational presence. The new presence in his theory is no potential presence that awaits the development of the mystical life to render it actual.

But does he so emphasize the ontological aspect as to neglect the new character, the supernatural character of the divine indwelling? Not even his severest critics have suggested this. The divine inhabitation of course involves also a true possession and not merely a new presence. Has de la Taille stressed this less well than the objective theorists? Far from neglecting this aspect, it has been shown to offer the only solid basis for a genuine objective theory. For in de la Taille, before any act of the just soul, the soul is instructed with the power to love God as God loves himself, since the soul is formally assimilated to God as he is in himself, assimilated in a way impossible in any theory that denies actuation of the soul.

Possession between spiritual beings is had by knowledge and love. By the union of grace as actuation man "has" God. He "has" the divine substance in common with God. He possesses God in such wise that he may, according to the thomist dictum, "freely use and enjoy him". When God creates the human soul he creates an image of himself capable of possessing God in an imperfect way. God represents himself in the natural soul in a similitude, not according to his proper spirituality and intellectuality. It belongs to efficient causality so to assimilate the effect to the cause by a likeness or similitude. Consequently the created, natural image of God has not the power to know and to possess God in a fashion similar to God's own knowledge and love of himself. Its spirituality is not that proper to God himself. That kind of spirituality is given to it by grace, where the unique formal causality at work in the production of grace assimilates the soul to the proper perfection of the quasi-formal cause, God. The proper effect of formal causality is to assimilate, not to a likeness of the cause, but to the proper perfection of the cause.

We might say then that although God is present to the soul before the advent of grace he is not properly speaking "possessed" by the soul before the advent of grace and the Uncreated Gift. The natural soul cannot attain to God as the Son attains to the Father, cannot enjoy God in the fashion that God enjoys the divine perfections. It is destined rather to enjoy God as God is found in his creaturely similitudes. No new effects of efficient causality can, by addition one to another, alter the nature of this incapacity for "possession" or order the soul efficaciously to God as he is in himself.

Quasi-formal causality, assimilating to the very nature of God effects the transformation and gives the capacity to possess. In the gift of grace God truly gives himself and giving, is possessed in a way that is impossible without the giving. It is the Self-communication that is implied in grace as actuation by Uncreated Act.

Ultimately, as the "action" of God in creation is and will remain profoundly mysterious, so the activity of God in actuating the just soul is and will remain a mystery. It is a reflection of the mystery of the Divine Essence itself. When we have come to this door we can only stand in awesome silence before the height and the depth of the incomprehensible ways of God.

NOTES

1 Morency, *op. cit.*, pp. 239-240, n.